Confessions of a Serial Entrepreneur
Challenges—Mistakes—Triumphs

en·tre·pre·neur
ˌäntrəprəˈnər/
noun
noun: **entrepreneur**; plural noun: **entrepreneurs**

1. a person who organizes and operates a business or businesses, taking on greater than normal financial risks in order to do so.

***

Sprinkled throughout this narrative; lessons are illustrated that when you are eager to learn and not fearful of making mistakes, positive things will happen for you.

This book is a retrospective diary of the author's business experiences starting, selling, licensing, and collapsing twenty business ventures over a span of 70-plus years from Massachusetts to California and some states in between.

There are successes, failures, and a few abandoned "good ideas" along the way; but lessons can be learned for anyone considering an entrepreneurial enterprise for themselves, a relative, friend or a business associate.

Author Bill Effinger, born in Duluth Minnesota shortly after the great depression hit will be 87 years young on August 4th 2017.

A Snapshot Autobiography:

I am a self-taught 'out-of-the-box' thinker and innovator/pioneer; I have exceled in marketing and management techniques, a published writer in several national magazines and newspapers, author of 18 published Essays and eight books.

At age 13, I and my younger brother lost our father when he was accidentally shot to death by a careless hunter. As a result, our mother was forced to go to work for survival. Three years later, we moved to Michigan where mom had sisters and a brother.

I worked that summer as a hod-carrier for a plastering contractor. Not wanting to return to school in September, I decided to follow my father's dream of moving to California, so I set my future in motion—leaving home at age 16 heading alone to California on a Greyhound bus, which is where and when my adult life began.

After spending a year working for Sears in their stock room and display department in Inglewood, I enlisted in the Navy at age 17, took their GED Exam receiving very high marks and was issued my high school diploma. That is the extent of my formal education.

After my discharge from the Navy in 1950, I entered the building, construction, and development field, as an apprentice carpenter at age 20, becoming a journeyman and licensed contractor within three-years.

Elected to the City Council and appointed Mayor of the City of Buena Park, California, at the age of twenty seven, one of my accomplishments as mayor was promoting the City of Buena Park's sponsorship of sending a Little League team to play baseball in the cities of Tokyo, Japan and Seoul, Korea in conjunction with President Eisenhower's newly formed "People to People" program in 1958.

Many times over the years, I have been an invited guest lecturer for several universities and colleges in different states on the subjects of business ownership, personnel management and entrepreneurship, sharing my experiences with hundreds of individuals desirous of owning their own business.

As a consultant for the past 35 years I have helped numerous failing companies in several states survive and become profitable.

※※※

Confessions of a Serial Entrepreneur

Challenges—Mistakes—Triumphs

Bill Effinger

New Century Publishing

20391 Fortune Place NE

Poulsbo, Washington 98370

All rights reserved including the right to reproduce this book in any form including digital copies in any form whatsoever.

This book produced in the United States of America.

Copyright © Bill Effinger 2017

All Rights Reserved

ISBN-13: 978-1544284828

ISBN-10: 1544284829

Cover Design

Bill Effinger

Other Books/Essays by the Author

Books

Making Crime Pay—How Identity Thieves Steal Your Money

I Told You So

Memories—An Eighty year Retrospective

The Vortex Made Me Do It

When You Can't Find a Job-Create One

Revolution 2012 –A Citizens War Against Congress

The Best Way to Manage People is—DON'T

Remembrances & Ruminations

Revolution 2016—The Trump/Sanders Earthquake

Essays

First Train Ride

Midnight Duel

Adventure in the Antipodes

More Guns—Less Crime-A Rebuttal

America—The Challenge and The Race

My Big Dream

Snippets of a Life

CONTENTS

A Chronological History of Bill Effinger's Businesses

Speedy Quick Delivery Service 1950	PAGE 9
Boulevard Saw Shop 1950: sold in 1952	PAGE 11
W.R. Effinger Rough Framing Company 1951-1956	PAGE 14
Decca Investors Inc. 1957:	PAGE 19
S & S Construction Company: 1957-1961	PAGE 25
W.R. Effinger Designer Builder 1957-1961:	PAGE 28
Alamitos Belmont Corporation 1961-1968:	PAGE 32
College Park Realty 1960-1971	PAGE 33
Community Plaza: 18 Condominium bldgs... 1966	PAGE 34
Rancho Valencia: 234-unit Apartment Complex 1966-1971	PAGE 37
Valencia Liquors 1967-1971	PAGE 43
Rancho Valencia Continued	PAGE 46
Blue Bird Nursery 1968-1971	PAGE 51
Huntington Harbor liquors 1969-1971	PAGE 54
Valley View Appaloosa Ranch 1971-1981	PAGE 56
My Ten Years with Shapell Industries 1971-1981	PAGE 67
New Dimensions for Living 1981-1984	PAGE 73

Bill Effinger

Techno Data Inc. 1984	PAGE 84
Builders Construction Software 1985-1987	PAGE 88
Bird Construction Software 1987-1992	PAGE 91
Builders Marketing & Management Inc. 1992	PAGE 97
Fine Line Creations Greeting Card & T-shirt Designs	PAGE 105
WRE Consultant 1993-2008	PAGE 110
New Century Consulting: 2008 to Present	PAGE 118
My Management Philosophy	PAGE 122
It's a Family Thing: Several family members are entrepreneurs	PAGE 126
Summary of Challenges, Mistakes & Triumphs	PAGE 130
Afterword	PAGE 136

***

Foreword
Confessions of a Serial Entrepreneur

According to ancient mythology, the bird, *Phoenix*, is associated with the Sun and obtains new life by arising from the ashes of its predecessor. In more modern times, reference is often made to individuals who have experienced various degrees of success, only to then experience some degree of failure, but then rising up to achieve success once again as a "Phoenix." My father, Bill Effinger, in my estimation, is quite possibly the poster "child" for a modern Phoenix.

In this tome my father relates how at age of thirteen his Dad was accidentally killed by a careless hunter. This family tragedy had an immediate impact on my father's mother, his younger brother, and of course on him. Without a father of his own, he had to find various work to help sustain his small, young, mid-western family. His quest for work, then a career path, led him on a journey he could never have anticipated at thirteen. That part of the story and the varied, remarkable experiences that ensued, up to and including today, are best told by him within the pages that follow.

Many of the entrepreneurial adventures encapsulated in this riveting guidebook for success, of course, I am quite familiar with. As the second of four Effinger children, I lived through much of the early years and have witnessed and/or participated in to one degree or another. However, there are also things I learned for the first time or now understand more clearly.

During the course of his personal journey, as you will read, our father has experienced many more successes than setbacks. But, he learned valuable lessons from both, as he explains at the end of each chapter. He has had enough such experiences that they could fill more than several lifetimes. In fact, he has said to us more than once that he made a conscious decision long ago to live two lives – his own, and that of his deceased father, who died at such a young age. Here he achieved total success.

Bill Effinger

Although there is a commonality running through most of his career experiences in terms of being involved in and around the real estate and construction industries, they are quite varied and certainly not the same. But, a common thread intertwined in all is the fact that he was never afraid of the risks involved, nor short on desire, but had the courage of his convictions, embraced hard work, and was determined to succeed. Napoleon Hill, the author of *Think and Grow Rich*, said that desire is the starting point of all achievement. He was right, of course, but it is hard work and perseverance that ultimately get you to your goal.

At some point I can imagine that the reader will come to ask her/himself, "Wasn't any particular business or job fulfilling, rewarding or successful enough to offer abundance that would preclude moving on to other things?" A great question.

I believe our father is the most engaged and energized when he faces new challenges -- challenges that seem daunting to others. Some "challenges" arouse due to unforeseen circumstances, while others were engaged that offered potential opportunities but were, by their nature, to become temporary. Market forces, the economy, emerging technologies, less than honest actors and other forces were also at play. But regardless of the reasons for "moving on," the point my father makes is to keep moving *forward*. To not only survive, but thrive under whatever circumstances arise. That is paramount for the true entrepreneur.

Bill Effinger, although he lost his father when he was still a young boy, has had many mentors throughout his memorable life. And, while he achieved much success, he knows he did not take the journey alone. In turn, he has been a mentor to many, many others over several decades... including his three sons and only daughter. For that we owe him more than we can possibly repay. That mentoring quality was surely the driving force behind the intimate sharing with the reader of his experiences, lessons, and confessions. Our dad's father, Francis Effinger, would be very proud of his son. Enjoy.

Lynn Effinger
March 28, 2017

Speedy Quick Delivery Service

AGC7 Mount McKinley

The above Photo is the ship I served on as Radioman 3rd Class when at sea with **TACRON III** Tactical Air Control Squadron, when otherwise stationed at North Island Naval Base in San Diego California. I was discharged December 29, 1949 just before the Korean War. The ship was the command ship for General McArthur for the beginning of the conflict.

***

What does a twenty year old, married Navy Seaman 2nd class with a baby on the way, consider doing to sustain his wife and child and make his way in the world as he leaves the comfort of steady pay ($60.00 per month)? Why start a new business of course!

With a few months of Navy back pay, my new wife and I rented a small flat in Inglewood California in back of a garage repair shop. Accepting a family friend's offer to sponsor me in the carpenters' union as an apprentice, I went to work pounding nails on roofs of new homes being built for returning veterans of the Korean War, as well as veterans of World War II, using their GI Bill benefits to buy a new home.

But that was a five day a week job—there were still two other days in the week. Why not put them to work?

For whatever reason, which I can no longer remember, I had convinced myself that small mom and pop businesses needed a personal delivery system for their phone-ordered products to customers who had limited means of transportation.

My transportation acquired when leaving the Navy, was a pickup truck, so armed with my idea and no fear, I began to visit local small businesses extolling the virtues of using my services to deliver their purchased products to the buyer for a small fee.

Enter: "Speedy Quick Delivery Service"

After a few weekends of soliciting with limited success, I ventured into the Pep Boys store in the neighboring city of Hawthorn.

The company had just begun a major promotion of selling the new wonder of entertainment, Television sets, in a variety of sizes and shapes. The manager of the department told me he would use my services but only if I was exclusive to his department.

Having no Speedy Quick clients as yet, the decision was easy. We made an arrangement where I would deliver the TV's on weekends for a fee based on miles to and from the delivery points and I was in business—for a short time.

After a few months and for reasons never explained to me, there was a falling out between the TV sales division and the auto parts division of Pep Boys, and TV sales were stopped.

With the ending of the Pep Boys, TV sales, Speedy Quick ceased to exist as it became obvious that my idea which seemed good at the time wasn't received by the Mom and Pops' of the time with equal

Fortunately, my job as an apprentice carpenter was my income and all I lost was time and some pride of having to abandon my idea.

Lesson learned—research your idea before implementing it and investing time, effort and finances. Mistakes in business ventures can be costly and hard to recover from. This was not a failed business, it was a lesson learned and shared.

Boulevard Saw Shop 1950: sold in 1952

My burning desire to have my own company continued to simmer with each nail I pounded during my day job of carpentering. The booming after-war years of building new homes for returning veterans using the GI Bill's no down payment option was providing me a working wage, but I wanted more.

Flipping through the pages of one of my favorite magazines one evening, I spotted an enticing advertisement from Foley Industries, touting the freedom of owning your own business by buying their saw and lawn mower sharpening equipment.

Everything one needed to start a thriving business was being offered for immediate delivery on a monthly payment plan. Next step, convince my wife this would be a good idea to pursue.

With wifely acquiescence, I took the next step—finding a suitable place to open our new business where she would have to be during the day while I worked my day job.

Almost miraculously we found the perfect spot; a tiny about 200 square foot store fronting on Hawthorne Boulevard in Torrance where we were living. I don't recall the rental rate, but we rented the space on a month-to-month agreement, and I contacted the Foley Company, ordering their sharpening equipment.

While we waited for delivery of the equipment, I designed, built, painted and hung a sign depicting a large circular saw blade with "Boulevard Saw Shop" in the center and took a picture, now long gone.

Electric powered Skill Saws were the predominant power tool being used in construction, which were provided by framing contractors for use by their carpenter employees, and each saw would go through at least one saw blade a day and many times two or three, depending on what they were being used for.

Carpenter crews of fifty, a hundred or two-hundred was not unusual for those booming years, and that was a lot of blades to be sharpened.

So I did the natural thing, I approached my job foreman and solicited the company's business of sharpening their blades. The sharpening equipment also included a machine for sharpening hand saws, so I let everyone on the job site know I would sharpen their hand saws when they became dull.

I made another sign and placed it in the window of our new shop that read 'We sharpen Lawn Mowers' and our phone number.

Soon all of our ordered equipment arrived with set-up instructions and directions on how to use the equipment and we were in business.

The plan was that my wife would be in the store answering the phone taking orders and deal with walk-ins during the day from noon until I got home from my day job, I would then sharpen the saws and mowers until finished with the promised delivery schedule.

And that worked until the rain came, and came, and came. Unfortunately, in Southern California when it rains, working outside isn't possible. Not just because of the wet, but the mud, which is thick, sticky adobe type soil nearly impossible to walk in.

The good news was that I could spend all day working in our sharpening shop. The bad news was there wasn't enough business to sustain us.

Just about the time the carpenter work shut down, Northrop Aircraft began a hiring blitz. Needing something to keep us from going broke; I was hired and quickly moved from being a riveter to an inspector when my plan-reading skills were noted.

The beauty of my new job in the factory was it was the swing shift, meaning I went to work at 4pm and worked until midnight, which left me able to work in the shop from 8am to 3:30pm, and that kept the money coming in.

When the rain quit and the sun came out drying everything up, my life became a bit hectic. I reported to my construction job at 7:00am; rushed home to change clothes and get to Northrop by 4pm, then swing by the saw shop at a few minutes past midnight to sharpen saws.

This routine lasted for about a year until exhausted, we decided to sell the shop.

I promised the new owner I would do my best for the new owner in keeping saw blades coming his way, but he should seek new jobsites, which he did.

So that business experiment ended on a positive note. I didn't get rich, but I had the experience of owning and operating my own business successfully.

Lesson learned: Owning your own business is fun, profitably rewarding and hard work. Know your market, get to know your clients and serve them well; they will continue to use your services and most likely recommend you to others.

***

W.R. Effinger Rough Framing Company 1951-1956: Dissolved

My work ethic on jobsites as a rough framing carpenter rewarded me with advancement to job foreman and superintendent, allowing me to meet more tradesmen and expose me to possible opportunities in the business.

One such opportunity was learning how to estimate direct labor time as a cost to a framing job for each of the processes we were using in constructing an entire building; In this case, a single family home.

Soon I was itching to start my own framing company, but I had no contacts with independent General Contractors with whom I would need to attempt to get their framing work; but as a job superintendent, I had made friends with some of our material supplier field represenntatives.

However, California state law requires a license to bid and enter into any contract, so my first step was to get a license which required taking a test.

Framing Contractor fell under the designation of General Contractor, (GC) so if I took and passed the test, I could not only bid and contract for framing jobs, I could also contract for the entire project if I chose—but I wasn't ready for that—yet.

A few years earlier, I had to take a test to go from Apprentice to Journeyman Carpenter, so several of the questions in the GC exam were similar, but it was a tough test, which I did pass on the first attempt.

License in hand, I approached the Salesman who represented the Sun Lumber, the largest lumber dealer in Southern California at the time, who ultimately became one of my best business friends, and asked him for names and introductions to some general contractors building individual homes one at a time.

With a list of potential contractor clients in hand, the first thing I needed to do was line up a crew who I could count on as being hardworking, knowledgeable of more than one element in the framing process, and willing to go to work with me on an on-call basis until I could line up enough work to keep a crew busy every day of the week.

My plan was to pay above Union scale wages—I along with many others in the field were breaking the Union rules by piece-working (being paid by the job, rather than by the hour) and most framing contractors were ignoring the rules because there was so much work and competition, the unions just looked the other way—if they didn't they would lose their members.

Within a few weeks, I had a sufficient number of men willing to take a chance with me, so I felt confident in seeking my first contract.

***

Getting the first contract didn't take long, but now I had to not only work with my crew as one of them, I had to find the next contract, so we could move smoothly from one to the other without losing days in between, otherwise my crew wouldn't stay with me.

Things fell into place quite well as more contractors were introduced to me and several of them had more than one house to build in their pipeline.

Within the first year, I had enough jobs going that I need a second crew, and then I was introduced to an apartment builder, which expanded my crew needs.

More crews meant more equipment needs, and so it went. My jobs were going smoothly, my men were making more than they could elsewhere, as I paid bonuses on every contract relative to speed of completion and the cost relative to what I had bid—Life was good.

Beginning the fourth year of my business, an opportunity was presented to me that was enticing. A friend of mine was a superintendent for a well-known builder who was about to build 100 homes and he said he would help me get the job if I could give his builder a competitive bid.

I told my friend that the job would require my purchasing more equipment, lining up a larger number of framers than I had and I didn't have enough finances to carry the size of payroll I would need.

My friend told me he would get back to me to see if he could work something out.

A few days later, my friend asked me to meet him on the new jobsite which was being graded and would soon be ready for foundations.

Arriving at the site, my excitement of the possibility that I might be framing a hundred houses here and that could launch me into a bigger game, overpowered my good judgement as my friend explained that the builder would carry the payroll, including my pay each week, and at the end of the job, all non-expended funds left after paying payroll taxes would be paid to me in one lump sum.

I accepted his offer and asked to have it put in writing and I would start lining up framing crews to be ready when the time came.

Excitedly, I drove to the hardware store I had been buying all of my equipment from and ordered the tools I thought I would need, adding the order to my account. Because the purchase was so large, it had to be approved by upper management, but I was cautioned that I needed to stay current or my credit would be cut off.

I then began lining up framers giving them the projected start date of the job and getting assurances they would come when I called.

When the call came we were ready to build the planned 100 houses at the rate of two completely framed houses per week. And we did. On time, on budget with a nice check waiting for me on completion day—or so I thought.

I submitted my bill for the balance owed based on my tracking of the payroll paid and the full contract balance with expectations of receiving my check the next day. Instead, I was told the builder's accountant was doing a recap and it would be "a few days".

A few days stretched into a week and then I got mad as well as worried. My friend had no answers except to say he was sorry and then my phone calls ceased to be answered.

I drove to the office of the builder and waited in the lobby for someone, anyone to tell me what was going on, but nobody showed up.

Now I couldn't even reach my friend.

***

My crew leaders urged me to get lawyers involved which by now was an obvious but scary thought. Not having a clue where to turn, I went to the Yellow Pages (almost a collectors' item today) and picked a firm which sounds like something out of a Hollywood comedy. But who knows, a lawyer is a lawyer, right?

So I called the firm of 'Wilde and Wooley'; I'm not kidding! Wilde and Wooley Attorneys at Law in Torrance, California were about to become the first attorney firm I ever hired. Unfortunately it wasn't the last, but that's for a later story in this book.

My first meeting was with both partners, after which Wilde was assigned the task which I found apropos, because I was wild with anger and scared to death. I was about to fight for what was right, but soon found that right, doesn't always win.

Naturally concerned about cost for my representation, the lawyers gave me a 'not to exceed' number, along with the assurances that they understood the situation and would not drag the issue into court—so much for that—we ended up in court and not only lost but were basically made fools of.

The contract turned out to favor the builder in the fine print—always read the fine print, and when the Judge greeted the opposing attorney with "Nice to see you again", I knew the ball game was over—and it was.

Obviously, we lost, I had to pay the attorneys and my business was delivered a fatal blow.

Very chaste and despondent, I assessed what had happened, where I was and what I was going to do next. During the whirlwind of my growing business, we purchased a new home in Buena Park in Orange County, California, rented our home in Torrance, incurred some new debt to furnish the new home and bought a new car—under those circumstances, not good.

What to do?

***

Bill Effinger

What not to do was panic. Assessing the damage, all I had lost was the promised payday at the end of the job. I had received my paycheck every week along with my crew. I had purchased a great amount of equipment which I could dispose of, albeit at a loss, but under the terms of the original agreement with the builder, his company had paid for most of it, so this wasn't the end of the world either.

The biggest loss was to my pride, but I deserved it. I plunged into something I wasn't ready for, and I paid the price. I made a mistake. I was 26 years old, learned a lesson the hard way and, healthy and able to tackle the next thing life had in store for me.

So—onward and upward to my next business venture.

After note to this story: The builder was later indicted for income tax evasion and fled to Italy, his home country, after all of his assets were seized by the U.S. Treasury. Several years later he turned up in Mexico trying to settle with IRS for 10-cents on the dollar.

Lesson learned: When opportunity knocks, do your homework; assess the opportunity for what it is, read the fine print. Should the contract you are being asked to sign have clauses you don't understand, seek legal advice and proceed with caution. Should the need for legal advice arise at some point in the execution of your contract, make sure the lawyer or law firm you engage, has specific experience in the type of issue you are confronted with.

***

Decca Investors Inc. Dissolved: 1957-1958

Recovering from my wounds caused by the debacle of my framing business took some time, but I had to do something to bring in some money.

My choices were to start beating the bushes for new work as a framing contractor or do something different.

Shortly after moving to Buena Park, I had joined the Junior Chamber of Commerce and became very active in the organization. The opportunity to meet other young men of my age, all getting started in life with their wives and small children was very helpful for me.

Many of the JC members, most, actually, had jobs leaning to the professional side; lawyers, bankers and sundry other professions. Very few were blue collar types, which at this point in my life I considered myself to be, even though I had owned my own business. I still swung a hammer with my crew when I wasn't hustling new jobs.

Somewhat disillusioned from the recent experience, I checked the help wanted ads and noticed that my alma mater Northrop was hiring in their Santa Ana location where they were working on government contracts for weapons.

Based on my positive history with the company previously, and proven skills of understanding mechanical drawings connected airframes, I was hired and given the title of 'Engineer' of all things—a bit of a stretch, but I took it.

Now I would go to work in a white shirt, tie and sport coat and could consider myself 'one of the guys' in the JC's. The best part was I wouldn't have to be worried about making payroll every week. I would be getting a check instead.

***

Just shy of a year, my doorbell rang at my home and one of my very best friends and former member of my framing crew was standing there. Bob had been on my crew when I was a job foreman and when I started my framing business he was the first one to sign up and stayed with me right to the end.

He said he was desperate, he needed work but he couldn't get hired unless he had a framing partner for a big subdivision of homes being built in La Mirada, just North of Buena Park and pay was almost double what I was making at Northrop.

We talked for a couple of hours and I told him I would let him know the next day. I was enjoying the job at Northrop, but the pay didn't compare to what I could make as a framer. My Santa Ana coworkers were mixed. We all got along very well and I enjoyed the atmosphere, but the money was a big factor. Quitting Northrop twice would surely keep me from ever being hired again.

After discussing things with my wife, I called Bob and said I would be his partner. The next day I was back in jeans with a hammer on my hip and working like a beaver.

***

Buena Park was a small town, dominated by Knott's Berry Farm to the south on Buena Park Boulevard, and on the North end of the boulevard was a Hunts Tomato packaging plant. I sensed that change was coming and the boulevard was going to become busy with commercial development.

One afternoon returning from work I noticed a for sale sign on a vacant parcel of land fronting on the Boulevard, so out of curiosity I called the Realtor and asked the price, which I don't recall now, but it seemed to me to be underpriced for what I was sure the land would be worth in a few years.

I called a friend of my mother's, who was a land planner and told him about the parcel and my thoughts on it being an investment opportunity. I asked if he might check it out, which he did, and agreed that it was an opportunity.

I mentioned this to a couple of my JC friends, who seemed interested, so I decided to look for ten people willing to invest enough money that we could buy the property, with the idea of holding it until it increased in value and then sell.

The response I received was positive enough that I filed incorporation papers for Decca Investors, Inc. planning to find nine investors who would pool their money so we could buy the property. My mom's friend was one of the investors. I structured the plan so that my one-tenth share was paid for by the other nine, and my job was to manage the investment until it was time to sell.

We didn't have to wait long. About nine months later, a very large parcel contiguous to our parcel was purchased by a major commercial developer with intentions of building a shopping center—Bingo!

Once the developer received commercial zoning for his project, our land value doubled—in my view it was time to sell; but my partners didn't agree. They wanted to retain the property feeling it would become more valuable if we waited.

We argued for several weeks as I showed them what I believed was the strategy for buying and selling land even though I had never done this before. I couldn't win them over, so I said I wanted them to buy me out. They would pay me my one tenth share based on the value at the time of my buyout and they could hold it as long as they wanted. They agreed and we parted, I was happy and they were happy.

The nine investors held the property for four more years and the property increased a little bit, but nowhere near the return on what they could have made by selling when I wanted to and reinvesting the money.

Once the property was sold Decca Investors was dissolved and everybody was happy. My life was going to take another unexpected change.

My experience of buying and selling land for the past 70-years has shown that when purchasing real estate, especially land, and zoning changes from a long standing dormant condition such as agricultural to commercial the value rises instantly to its

highest and best use value. From that point on, the value will only rise relative to the general economy and inflation.

***

As the months rolled by, my involvement in the JC's got deeper and I became a member of the board of our club, and then a State Director. The outgrowth of this was my increasing interest in politics.

Winning the speaking contest at the JC's state convention, in 1956, got the attention of some political activists and the next thing I knew, I became a candidate for the Buena Park City Council race in 1957.

Here I was, pounding nails and lifting framed walls during the day, and campaigning for public office in the evening—tiring but exciting.

Unknown to me at the time, my Mother's friend, the land planner, had mentioned me to one of his builder clients that they might want to meet with me because they were looking for someone to locate and help buy land suitable for developing homes. He told them the story of Decca Investors and my theory of value.

I won the election and was appointed mayor by the council, making me the youngest mayor in the U.S. at age 27 I was told.

Shortly thereafter, I was contacted by the builder client of my mom's friend and a meeting was set.

Confessions of a Serial Entrepreneur

Mayor Travis Announces He Will Run for Council

Four Will Try for 2 City Posts

One would like to make the best impression when being interviewed for a potential job, but unfortunately for me the day and time of the meeting was set in Beverly Hills, for the same Saturday as the Buena Park Pioneer Day Parade at a time which meant I would have to go directly to the meeting with no time to change clothes.

I was dressed in full cowboy regalia including my Stetson hat, and topping it off I was meeting two Jewish brothers, survivors of the concentration camps, driving my German Karrmann Ghia! Unfortunately as I pulled up to the office on La Cienega Boulevard, both Shapell brothers were just getting out of their car looking right at me and my red car—talk about a first impression!

The meeting went well in spite of the side issues of the car and my clothes. I answered all their questions and was told I would hear from them in a few days.

I did hear from them and after negotiating my salary, I agreed to start in two weeks as S & S Construction Company's land buyer and whatever else they might find for me to do.

My life now took a turn which I had never expected, but was eager to learn and excel at whatever challenges were put in front of me—and there were many. Accepting the position of land buyer with the Shapell Brothers set the stage for the seventeen businesses I would start over the next fifty years, which are incorporated in this book replete with lessons learned from all, both good and bad.

✱✱✱

Lesson learned: Sometimes the seemingly littlest things can become monumental in the overall scope of your life. Using what we were taught as youngsters: "Stop, Look and Listen" for oncoming traffic, can also be used when confronting an opportunity presented when least expected.

S & S Construction Company Land Buyer

One of the gifts I was born with is that I can envision completed buildings from a roll of plans, in three-dimension when I am looking at terrain on which those buildings might be placed. I'm sure some of this was enhanced when I studied drafting and mechanical drawing in junior high school. Isometric drawing was part of our curriculum. This talent helped me when I undertook the task of being a land buyer for my new employer.

I spent the next four years adding responsibilities to my land acquisition activities after a very fortunate land find within the first 60-days on the job made me look like a hero.

Prior to my joining the company, almost all of the company's projects were in Downey and Paramount—small cities with many dairies. As the dairy farmers moved further east, seeking to get away from the growing cities, builders would buy up the dairies and build their homes.

I was very familiar with Orange county cities, so my first search turned into a gold mine for the company; a very large parcel of land nestled in a gentle rolling valley that would accommodate several hundred homes, for an unbelievably low price per acre compared to what the company had been paying.

Soon I was poking my nose in other areas, either by request or just seeing what might be needed. Not long after being there I discovered a problem that needed correcting. The homes we were building were all VA or FHA financed and both agencies took a dim view of construction defect complaints from their buyers.

S & S was building quality homes: solid, well designed, lath and plaster and hardwood floors throughout. But nothing is ever perfect, and some complaints would come in. The problem was that's all that was happening. The complaints would come in and sit there with no action being taken.

David was the younger brother and second in command, Nathan was the CEO, short in stature with a legendary temper. Brave person that I was I approached him and told him the complaints were out of control and we needed a system. Nathan's first instinct was to scream at whoever might be considered to be responsible for the issue at hand. All that did of course was make sure nobody ever told him of a problem.

There were drawers full of complaint slips, some several months old, which I showed both brothers, volunteering to fix it. The biggest issue for the brothers Shapell was how much my plan was going to cost them. My answer required one of the best sales pitches I ever made, but it worked.

I convinced Nathan that once we had the program in motion that I was going to design, as the word got out, we would soon sell houses based on our customer service reputation. With the help of David after a few screaming sessions, Nathan gave me the go ahead.

The most effective aspect of the plan, played to Nathan's strength—he was a hands-on leader, feared by his team in the field and in the office. So, to make the customer service plan work, our customers were told if they didn't get satisfaction, they could call Nathan direct and he would talk to them. We told the field crew what we were telling the homeowners, which had the effect of insuring the complaints would get action or they would have the wrath of Nathan all over them.

Ultimately the company was honored in the Congressional Record for our excellence in customer service and the company's reputation soared, many times selling to second and third-time buyers and their families.

I left S & S and started my own building company in 1962. It took Nathan 10-years to forgive me.

Lessons learned: The owner of the company, Nathan Shapell allowed me to seek my own level of responsibility while never allowing accountability to wane, which proved to me that when you are eager to learn and not fearful of making mistakes, positive things will happen for you.

The result was that I applied that philosophy to all of my future endeavors.

The following pictures were taken on Look-back trip to Buena Park. The one immediately below is on the Buena Park City Hall Entrance Wall where all mayors up to that period are on display—the years do take their toll.

Bill Effinger

W.R. Effinger Designer Builder 1957-1961

Before leaving S & S, we purchased a home in Long Beach in one of our subdivisions Named College Park, enrolled our three boys in school, then I decided to start my building company.

Long Beach had an older residential section of homes built in the 30's. The area had been up-zoned to medium density, which allowed the demolition of the older homes and the replacement of them with apartments. Most of the lots were 50 feet wide, 120 foot deep to a 25 foot alley in the rear.

There were several builders active in the area, most of them building the maximum allowed; eight to ten units with minimum allowable parking, not doing the neighborhoods any favors for living and parking conditions.

My business plan, after studying the area and talking to Realtors, was to build three or four attached units to a lot, one of them being a large "owners unit" with a four-car garage opening onto the alley, and market these to the GI's who had by now built a substantial equity in the VA/FHA home they had purchased when they returned from WWII. They were close to, or already retired; they could sell their existing home, move into my owners unit which was larger than most GI homes of that era, and rent out the two or three units which would pay the mortgage for the entire building.

Working from my home, I began scouting the area I wanted to focus on, which was close to an upscale area known as Belmont Park looking for homes for sale. It didn't take long. I located a lot that looked like a problem to most potential buyers, but it fit my concept perfectly.

I made an offer subject to getting bank approval and then ran to the Bank which had a reputation for smiling on builders. The result was that I was introduced to the bank manager who took a real interest in my concept, suggesting I fill out the required paper work and call him the next day.

The Banker told me he liked what I was doing, that he could make the lot purchase financing, but I would have to show him that I had "take out financing" so that he knew he would be paid back by a viable source. Noting the look on my face of "what do you mean" he gave me the name of a person at a local savings and loan who I should talk to.

So that's what I did. My new building business was off and running. With financing of the lot purchase secured and assurance of the loan to build the proposed project waiting for my construction drawings, I went right to work.

Putting my junior high school architectural drawing class studies to task, I set up a drafting board in my makeshift office and began the design of my first project—it wasn't easy because the lot I chose had a severe slope facing the street; but once I looked at the lot from an unconventional view (one of my more common traits) I saw the answer—carve the building into the slope.

That solution accomplished two things, reducing the silhouette of the building and allowing direct access to the tuck-under garage from the street which would be handy for owner and tenants.

***

After securing the building permit, I took the plans and permit to my construction/takeout lender, Belmont Savings & Loan, received their approval and began excavation of the site the following day. Before construction began I had a sign made that said: 'For Sale New Apartment Home, W.R. Effinger Designer Builder' with my phone number.

The lot faced a busy residential street with a name few ever pronounced correctly, 'Ximeno' which was a main access to the Northside of town from the Belmont Park neighborhoods. This street became pivotal in my business, where I added a few more of my owner home/apartment buildings and a development project that changed the trajectory of my building business and my future.

Within two-weeks a received several calls on the project, one of which developed into a sale of the yet to be constructed building—I was ecstatic, needless to say.

The purchasers fit the profile of my target market, with one exception; the man was a veteran, semi-retired, and father of two children, one of whom was a victim of Down Syndrome aged 23 and a son ready to leave home for college.

I couldn't have asked for a better family to experience my first project: they were interested in my concept; they were patient during construction as we made some changes they wanted to parts of the planned interior of their living unit and best of all, they agreed to allow me to show their building to prospective buyers of future buildings I planned to build.

Excited to share my good fortune with the banker that gave me the loan for the building I just sold, I stopped by the bank and to my surprise, he urged me to find another lot and he would give me a lone to purchase it with the same condition as the first, make sure I had a takeout loan.

Within a week I had a lot picked out just about a block away from the one I was currently building, around the corner on a side street. The banker made the loan and asked to see the plans when I had them completed.

A few weeks later, I took the plans of the new building, a four unit with parking in the rear under a top floor unit and an owners unit on the ground floor with a 20-foot set back and lawn in the front. This was to become a standard configuration for many such buildings for the next few years.

I brought the plans to the banker and he asked if he could keep them overnight, because he wanted to show them to his wife. Of course I agreed.

Returning the next day to pick up the plans, I got the shock of my life—the banker said he and his wife had looked at the location and wanted to buy the finished building depending on the price. After giving him what I planned to sell the unit for, he said "sold" and my yet to be started project was already sold!

I was clearly on a roll, so I stated looking for another lot to build on. This continued to happen with such regularity that it was hard to believe—I couldn't build this product fast enough. Soon I had such a system of finding a lot, buying it, demolishing the existing structure, then building the new home/apartments, it looked like it was never going to end.

One thing was happening that seemed to be self-defeating—each new lot purchase was costing more than the last; Realtors and the owners they were soliciting to sell were noticing my success, as my demolition contractor moved through the neighborhoods knocking down existing structures. My agreement with this contractor guaranteed demolition in one day, and he never failed me.

An interesting side note to this is I received a call from the title officer of the company guaranteeing title to the lenders, alerting me to the fact that they couldn't record the loan because some work had already begun on the home we were supposed to demolish that day. I was incredulous! That couldn't be—had my guy jumped the gun?

I rushed to the site and discovered that neighbors to the home to be demolished, knowing it was going to be destroyed, had gone into the home and begun dissembling fixtures and plumbing, tearing things up pretty well.

I immediately contacted the Realtor, told him what happened, and informed him his commission was in jeopardy and to tell all those neighbors that I was filing a police report and they would all be arrested.

Then it got funny. Slowly throughout that day and the next all of the appliances, sinks and toilets began a large pile in the front yard.

I notified the title company, they sent out their inspector, we recorded the loan the following day, and the house was demolished—end of calamity!

***

Lesson Learned: I plunged into my new business with the usual gusto and abandon that up to now had typified my life—I knew what I wanted to do, I felt I knew the market I was going to be building for and I knew where I was going to build my first products.

Everything fell into place with such ease, I didn't appreciate it at the time. The more buildings I constructed, the more I sold and the more I sold, the growth of the business was remarkable.

In retrospect, what I should have done was stop, take a breath and make a plan for the future—something I helped many of my clients do after I learned the lesson of hyper growth.

***

Bill Effinger

Alamitos Belmont Corporation

Growing as fast as I was, I needed some help, had outgrown my in-home office and needed a book keeper. I found a small commercial lot on 7th Avenue, the main access into Belmont Heights and built a two-story office building intending to lease the bottom floor and use the top for my office and a contract draftsman I had found to do my building plans in exchange for free rent.

At the same time of moving into the new building, I was advised to incorporate by a lawyer friend, so we created Alamitos Belmont Corporation. The name identified us as part of the Alamitos Bay and Belmont Shore, Park and Heights neighborhoods where most of our building activity was taking place.

Shortly afterward, my brother Jim joined me and I hired a book keeper who doubled as my secretary/assistant.

Before leasing the ground floor, we decided to create the real estate brokerage, "College Park Realty" principally to sell our buildings and acquire properties, thereby increasing our revenue by capturing commissions and cutting some costs.

Shortly after the move and forming the corporation, a new opportunity presented itself in the form of what would soon become somewhat history making for me and our little company.

***

Community Plaza-Long Beach California: Eighteen 3 & 4 Unit Buildings Sold: 1966-1971.

The rapid pace did start to slow just about the time that I became interested in what would be the next phase of my business.

I purchased two contiguous lots very close to Long Beach Community Hospital, which were too small for building my usual product, so I designed two duplex buildings with similar interior layouts: a duplex building with identical floor spaces sharing a common wall separating the units, designed to sell each unit as an undivided one-half of the whole. The title company agreed to issue title to each unit as long as there was a community agreement attached to the title. That resulted in quick sales of all four units.

Close to these two lots, was a large land parcel of about 5-acres. When I researched why the land was still undeveloped, I was told by city planners that the site had been used as a staging area for oil derrick building in the Signal Hill area, which was one of the largest oil producing properties in California.

Investigation with the title company proved to be problematic, in that there were many oil leases criss-crossing the property which would all have to be cleared before valid title could pass.

Undaunted and seeing a challenge which has always peaked my interest, I decided to visit the most feared planning director in Southern California, Werner Ruckti. His reputation was legendary. He chewed up and spit out more developers than anyone could count.

I called the planning office and arranged a meeting with the man, dropping the name of my former employer, S & S, who had and was building projects in Long Beach and had a very good reputation with city staff.

On the appointed day and time, I rolled up some drawing tissue, slid it under my arm and entered Mr. Ruckti's office. I was greeted with: "What can I do for you young man", as I was ushered to a seat across from him.

"Mister Ruckti I have an idea, and I'm going to need your help." That got his attention as I went on to tell him I was considering acquiring the land near the hospital and it had major problems, all of which I was willing to tackle, but the city was going to have to work with me and the title company to help clear up the issues.

Then I rolled out the tissue and made some quick outline of the site free-hand, and placed 18 squares within the outline and told him I wanted to place eighteen of my buildings I had been constructing and selling in the Belmont Park area.

Ruckti proceeded to tell me how he had always wanted to see that "eye sore" developed but nobody had ever been able or wanted to take the time or spend the effort.

Then I explained the other part of my plan: "I want to create a common community of buildings that will be owned by 18-individual owners, managed by a single entity, similar to the common ownerships in several buildings in Long Beach, but using a new technique that is being done in New York," I went on: "The term used for the concept is "condominium" which allows individual deeds to the properties, but singular to the specific owner, and all other parts of the property are deeded to a common interest association."

The man leaned forward, squinted at the drawings laid out on the tissue, then leaned back and said: "I like this; but you will have to show me that all of the legal hurdles and title issues can be resolved before you get too far: I will help you all I can, but all of the surrounding home owners will have to accept what you want to do—they have protested every plan proposed up to now."

After thanking Him profusely, I left Werner Ruckti's office buoyed by his acceptance to the idea and began the serious aspect of the project, which was to seek and hire a civil engineer to help create a viable set of subdivision drawings acceptable to the engineering department, and seek legal help on drawing documents that there was no precedent as yet in the state.

***

I had been attending seminars regularly, which were being presented by two lawyers from San Francisco, the subject of which was on real estate development issues and the projections of things to come in the industry. I was impressed, always taking copious notes, wanting to be as up to date as possible.

Based on a few interactions I had had with the seminar leaders, I decided to call them and see if they would help me with the condominium issue for my proposed project.

To my delight, they were interested in talking to me, and the rest is history on that subject. Not only did they help me with my project, they ultimately helped the state of California codify the Condominium Statute and I was developing the first ever condominium in the state of California—a memorable achievement.

Once I had the engineering drawings in my hands, I assembled some photos of the three and four unit buildings I had been erecting around town and began gowing door to door, selling the idea of my program to the prospective neighbors of my project, assuring them that what I was planning to do would increase the value of their property by getting rid of the eye sore and creating a new and well maintained community that I would create to be known as "Community Plaza".

As the weeks and months passed in the process of planning, designing, appearances before commissions and meeting with city building officials, my excitement was hard to control. That excitement was fueled with the fact that I was already receiving indications from prospective buyers, that there was going to be a ready market for the concept.

The project was built, sold and occupied within a year of breaking ground.

Lesson Learned: There are opportunities where others have not gone or have passed up. When things look difficult or maybe even impossible, the rewards for persistence and perseverance can be beyond your imagination. Follow your dream.

There is an after-story to all of this: After breaking ground for the unique ownership concept of Community Plaza. Over a period of several ensuing years, a well-known and very successful osteopathic surgeon who practiced at Long Beach Community Hospital ultimately became the single owner of all of the buildings in Community Plaza, purchasing each of them as they became available over the years.

Because of the way the original condominium ownership documents were drafted and recorded, should the surgeon decide to sell, he can sell the buildings individually rather than having to find a buyer for the entire project.

***

Rancho Valencia: 234-unit Garden Apartment complex 1966-1971: Relinquished

When we were nearing completion of Community Plaza, I was contacted by a Realtor© associate who said he had a property I might be interested in. The property was 20-acres located in the City of Garden Grove that had been a practice polo field for Hollywood actors and elites several years earlier.

I was very familiar with the city which was just a few miles from Long Beach, and one which I had experience with when I was with S & S, as we had built and sold several thousand houses there.

Acquiring a property that size was way out of my league, in my view at the time; but I agreed to check it out—nothing ventured, nothing gained.

The site fronted on the main street: "Garden Grove Boulevard", was as flat as you might imagine a polo field would be, and was just one block east of the main South to North access street from the freeway to the neighboring cities of "Stanton" and "Buena Park"— my former home, and the city I had been mayor of in 1957 and 1958.

Except for a large stand of Eucalyptus trees on the West side and the home of the owner, the site was ready to be built upon with very little site work.

Developing the site would require Planning and Zoning approval, which meant applying to the Planning Commission and City Council. I had a great deal of experience doing so when with S & S, and of course sitting with the Buena Park City Council, dealing with developers.

That experience served me well in that I learned one of the most valuable lessons of my entire development career; something too few builders and developers practice even today.

City staff and the commissions/councils they work for, have to perform for their respective communities in adhering to the city, county, state codes and ordinances. In rare cases when properly approached, are approvals denied. The action words here are *'properly approached'*.

Acknowledging the staff's position when first opening the discussion on a project by making them a part of the solution with a simple: "I need your help in working out what I want to do with this property and what you are required to ask me to do for approving this project" puts both the staffer and the developer on the same side of the table, working together to solve the issues in a very amicable, non-confrontational, and ultimately successful way.

After touring the site, I approached my primary lender, Belmont Savings and Loan and discussed the site and its potential with my loan officer, who had been working with me since my first building several years earlier.

I asked if they would consider doing this with me. The answer was to run the numbers come up with a plan for the site and we would discuss it—once again, nothing ventured, nothing gained.

***

After visiting the S & L, I made an appointment with the owner, who was 80 years old, sharp as a tack and an extremely wealthy heiress to her father's fortune. He was the original owner of most of the property now known as 'Signal Hill' where all of the oil was discovered and still being pumped. That was the good news.

The bad news was his instructions to the lady, his only child was, "never sell land—only lease it" Now that might be a problem.

Laying out some preliminary plans for the site, I used the maximum allowable density I could propose for the property, which had a two-zone use—commercial for the frontage on Garden Grove Blvd. and multi-density on the balance.

The result was 44 apartment buildings totaling 234 units in a garden style layout, plus 20 duplexes, a community/recreation building, 2 swimming pools and central pond, using my standard building and apartment types being sold in Long Beach, including the just completed Community Plaza.

The commercial site would have a two-story office building and three ground level retail buildings, assuming all of this would be approved by planning and council.

Developing residences on leased land was taking place in several places in Los Angeles and Orange Counties, and there was a distinct advantage to a lease versus having to purchase the land—the initial outlay of cash was minimal, relative to the land value. I no longer have the figures available, but assuming the cost might have been $2million, when that value is stretched out over 99-years at a cap rate of say 4-percent, the lessee (in this case my company) would have instant equity of the total value of their land, less the lease payments—a very big financial advantage .

There is also an advantage to the lessor in a land lease vs. a sale: Taxes are only paid as the annual rent comes in based on the amount of the payment, which is substantially less than when selling for a lump sum.

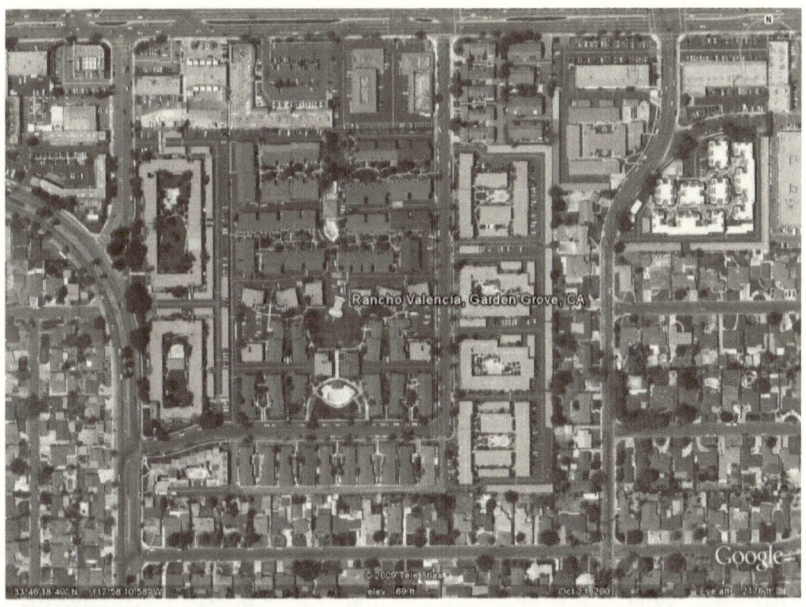

Based on the positive feedback from the lender, I made an offer for a 99-year lease with an option to purchase, subject to the approval of the project by the city and the lender providing the loans.

The owner accepted the offer and I hired a civil engineer to prepare the required drawings for submittal of the project to the city and the lender.

I developed a marketing plan that started with researching all of the existing apartments in the area and interviewing managers on what the rents were, and what amenities the apartments had in them and if there were other onsite amenities like pools, recreation rooms, etc.

I then developed some letters addressed to the tenants of all the competitors units, listing everything they didn't have, which we would have. We included a return envelope suggesting they get on the waiting list because we were taking reservations.

The apartment owners screamed and complained to the city and the Chamber of Commerce, but their complaints fell on disinterested ears.

By the time the first buildings were competed, we had more names than we had apartments available.

The marketing plan also set up a unique and never before done promotion. The title company provided me a chain of title that went back from our execution of the lease, all the way to the King of Spain. I had a calligrapher reproduce the document on a scroll, which along with a dozen Valencia Roses was handed to the tenant on move in. That made the news.

Construction was started on the commercial frontage for two reasons: to provide the public with a glimpse of the "California Rustic Spanish' tiled architecture we planned for the entire project, and to pre-lease as much of the commercial space as possible. Also, I wanted to get underway with building the store for my new enterprise, "Valencia Liquors".

Soon after construction started, I was contacted by a two-man partnership who wanted to put a new franchise business, "Taco Bell" into one of my buildings. Taco Bell was a new, but fast-growing enterprise and of course would help establish my convenience center.

There was a glitch to their request: Taco Bell wanted a free-standing building in the architectural style of all other Taco Bells being established everywhere. I refused to alter my planned style which consisted of broad overhanging clay tiled roof line extensions which acted as sun shading to reduce air conditioning costs for tenants, and a shaded walkway for shoppers.

Negotiations were at a standstill until the partners asked if I would meet with the founder of Taco Bell at his headquarters in Palos Verdes, California, an exclusive area South of San Pedro. The founder of Taco Bell was Glenn Bell—of course, why not?

Bell was affable but insistent on the free standing building; I was equally insistent. Bell was a bit younger than I was at the time, but not by much.

He explained that his expectant Franchisees were policemen and it could be an opening for other people on other police forces to become Taco Bell Franchisees.

I agreed to one alteration of my building plan: I allowed the familiar signature 'Bell Tower' vertical protrusion through the broad overhang that would be wrapping the building. Bell agreed to that change although reluctantly—so we had a tenant and he had a Franchisee—win win.

**

The two-story building we constructed adjacent to the rear of the liquor store housed our office, as we had increased the number of our employees substantially to cope with the number of projects underway.

My friend who was going to manage the store became my general manager with one eye on the store and the other on our building enterprise. With his help, we acquired an Arnold Palmer Dry Cleaning Franchise, which we located in the building adjacent to the Taco Bell—we felt that the number of tenants in our 234 apartment units would go a long way to sustaining the business and as it worked out it did—now I owned another business I hadn't planned on getting into.

When each apartment building was completed, we would notify those on our waiting list, which had grown exponentially, much to the chagrin of our competitors in the area, and our tenants would move into their new home (which is how we presented them) our apartments were "Apartment Homes".

Move-in day was a happy day for us and our new tenants when we presented them with a dozen red Valencia roses and the rolled up colored, calligraphic scroll, containing the chain of title from the

King of Spain, to lessen the rigors of their move. That got us a ton of publicity. We continued that program with every apartment home we completed until the last move in.

Lesson learned: Research the market and competition before designing your product to focus on what the competition is NOT offering their prospective purchasers or renters and when economically feasible, include those items and amenities in your product; doing so will allow an increase in price or rents.

***

Valencia Liquors

As the building process began with ground breaking and foundation pouring, a longtime friend of mine and former city manager of the city of Huntington Beach contacted me, asking if I would allow him to use the commercial address for his application to get a liquor license, and if he did get it, I could build his store and lease it to him.

Intrigued, I asked him what he had to do to get the license and he told me that he had to post $6,500.00 cash with the California Alcoholic Beverage Board and his name and posting number would be placed in the lottery when it was held. If his number was drawn, he would be issued a license.

I agreed, but with a condition that I would also post the cash to get a number. If his name was drawn, I would build him his store, but if I won and he didn't, I would build the store and he would manage it for me.

The property had 600-feet of frontage, so because the law stated that stores selling alcoholic beverages had to be at least 300 feet apart, I gave him an address on one side of the frontage and I took an address far enough away to allow us both to qualify.

When the drawing took place, my friend's name wasn't drawn, but mine was! Win some, lose some.

After several months, the project was approved by the city; our construction loan was approved and we began construction of the store, once all of the architectural drawings were approved.

Having visited liquor stores and never being impressed by their consistent tackiness, I set my goal of changing that for my new business.

Meeting with my friend whose idea it was to get a license, I explained what I wanted to do with the design and he was all for it.

The sale of alcoholic beverages in California was 'fair traded', meaning that retail markups were controlled by the ABC (Alcoholic Beverage Control Board). Mark up on all wines was 35% and hard liquor was 20%, so what seemed to be a natural to maximize profits, was boosting the sale of wine. Thus, the first 'wines of the world' feature and separate location within a store.

Next, I wanted the store to be a place where women weren't shy about shopping in my store, so elegance of the interior became part of my plan. High wooded and beam ceilings, red carpet and red clay tiles on the floor, brass trimming on the refrigerator moldings and shelves added to the ambiance, but the crowning feature came unexpectedly.

Back in those days, one could fly to San Francisco and back to San Diego for less than $20 Dollars, on PSA "Pacific Southwest Airlines", so we were frequent visitors of the "City on the Bay".

On one such trip, I noticed an advertisement that the city of San Francisco was dismantling its historical street lights and offering them for sale, so I purchased eight of them and shipped to the Garden Grove site.

The store was designed to have high, exposed-beams and sheathing ceilings. Two, 12" x 12" support posts were required to support the roof; they were placed in the center of the building. The ornate, black wrought-iron torchiere lights were mounted four to each post, providing light for the entire building, and many conversations of awe over the ensuing years. That of course was part of my marketing plan and strategy: Make the store memorable.

Much to the amazement of the many salesmen selling their products to the store, everyone to a person predicted it was a waste of money, were equally shocked at the dollar volume the store was producing in sales, our profits soaring equally.

One other issue that helped drive our bottom line was a wrinkle the ABC's ruling on markup: There was a provision that any store could sell a store brand (today's generic) alcoholic beverage at a 35% reduction from the branded item. Stores could then sell that product at a reduced price in competition with the branded variety.

Instead of following that line of marketing, I did the opposite. I created "Valencia Vodka" and "Valencia Bourbon", both Seagram brands then created very attractive labels with a beautiful Spanish woman dressed in a flowing red gown, wearing a black Tierra holding a bouquet of red Valencia roses—and marked the price above what Seagram was selling for—doubling my profit when sold.

That absolutely blew the Seagram salesman's mind when he saw the volume which those two products were selling—and delighted us with the commensurate profits.

Equally astounded were the wine salesmen, as wine snobbery had not yet entered the market place; but visiting our "Wines of the World" room was unique—bottles all laying corks facing out on their shelves and in the coolers, all displaying countries from around the world where they originated, low false ceiling with subdued lighting, all effects that drew people in—particularly the women.

When we opened the store we were overwhelmed with the response and it never stopped.

Lesson Learned: Follow your instincts, and only listen to professionals who represent the buying public rather than the companies they represent when selling you their products. Market researchers, local newspapers magazines, radio and TV ads are good sources, but there is nothing like good old fashioned asking questions of your friends, neighbors and associates on what they would like to see and experience in your product.

Being different than your competition has its rewards.

***

Rancho Valencia Continued

The project was rolling along very nicely, buildings were being completed, and tenants were moving in, the convenience center was under construction along with my liquor store and then disaster struck.......

Apparently the lender had violated their charter by making a loan on leased land; they panicked and stopped honoring my construction draws, which caused me to stop everything until we got things worked out—this was serious and totally unexpected.

The year was 1968, and the economy was spiraling downward and real estate was being hit hard as lenders were tightening the screws. (If this sounds familiar, it is. The cycle of ups and downs in real estate and the economy in general are unfortunately predictable, but few heed the warnings.

So what did the S & L do, when I had been borrowing and paying back millions of dollars for ten-plus years without a missed payment or never a single complaint from buyers or a mechanics lien ever filed?

Why of course, they stopped funding my construction draws and I couldn't pay my contractors and suppliers. Worst of all, years later when I confronted the former chairman of the S & L asking him why he did that to me when he had other builders and developers who had defaulted in different ways, his answer was dumbfounding.

He was now head of the California Savings and Loan Commission. And his answer: "I knew you would work it out because you were such a scrambler".

At that point I became very aware of why there were laws against carrying loaded guns. That was the closest I have ever come to experiencing in reality, the often quoted: "A good deed shall never go unpunished"; and I don't want to experience it again.

Meanwhile, back at the Ranch, I contacted the largest and most prestigious law firm in Long Beach: Ball, Hunt & Brown (the Brown being former Governor Pat Brown) and set up a meeting to see if they could help.

The first meeting yielded two things: first it was "a long shot" second; it was going to be expensive. The firm would not do anything until they received ten thousand dollars up front. Laying out that much when there would be little coming in was frightening, but I had no choice.

Before I agreed to give them the money, I wanted to understand what their proposed strategy was going to be.

First step would be giving them a history of my relationship with the S & L from the beginning; then a history on Rancho Valencia and all documentation for the loans and the underlying lease.

When they had reviewed all of the documents, they would draft a very large "Legal Brief", intending to scare the S & L enough that we would not have to file a suit. If a suit had to be filed, I couldn't afford the cost, so the "one shot" I had was going to have to be it.

The next step was for me to keep my ears close to my friends within the S & L to see what was going on between them and the state and if I could determine the most propitious time to put the Legal Brief in front of them.

Several weeks went by while I was holding meeting with my contractors and employees, telling them what I was doing and what was happening, assuring everyone that they would all get paid no matter what happened to me and the company: I kept my word. I listed all of the properties we owned, and then executed notes to each contractor on a property they chose in the value of the unpaid portion of their contract which they would hold until they were paid.

Approximately two-months later, my loan officer who was very embarrassed over what was happening contacted me and said the S & L was in negotiations with the state to perform a shot-gun wedding with another S & L in trouble. If/when Belmont agreed to the merger, the commission would cut them loose.

I alerted the law firm on the date I was given when the Belmont Board would be meeting; they drafted the Brief and on the scheduled day, a Marshal entered the board room and presented the two-inch thick Brief to the Chairman and left.

The law firm was contacted within an hour of delivery of the Brief, and a meeting was set up for the following day, to talk about what we wanted and what they were willing to do. They had to act fast, because their fate was in the hands of the state and my proposed action, outlined in the brief.

This was the biggest poker hand I had ever held in my life--- basically a pair of Duce's because I didn't have enough money to file the suit; but they didn't know that.

With my attorney sitting next to me in the meeting we sternly laid out our determination to take the case all the way—and it worked; partially.

Belmont agreed to complete the funding on all of the apartments under construction, but not the ten duplexes not yet started. I would have to find another lender for that. After consulting with the attorney, it wasn't what I wanted, but under the circumstances, we got that one shot, took it and had to accept that we won a lot more than what we could lose. My whole world would end if we couldn't finish those apartments, so we accepted the deal and we were back in business; But not for long.

***

The entire country was in a financial downturn. The banks and S & L's were losing money and forced mergers were happening daily, not as drastic as 2008, but bad enough to shake everyone up.

My local sources couldn't help, so I started looking to unconventional sources, ultimately finding a firm operating out of Beverly Hills California, Sononblick Goldman. The person assigned to me was a young man named George Smith, relatively new to his firm, but obviously he was a financial whiz; he ultimately took over the company, which is now: "George Smith Partners", George was quick on his feet, and he cut to the chase in a short period of time after touring my project and listening to my plight. "I can help you" he said—and he did.

As it turned out, the help we got turned out to be our ultimate downfall, and it was a wild ride in the process.

The final chapter of Rancho Valencia was written; we would meet and do business with former President John Kennedy's Press Secretary Pierre Salinger, who was the front man for United States Investment Fund (USIF), a high flying offshore real estate investment company, that was gobbling up large projects such as ours at a record pace around the U.S.

USIF, based in Miami Florida sent some of their officials to visit our project; they were duly impressed and within a few weeks we had their offer: they would fund the completion of the balance of the project for a 49% interest in the entire completed project, which we would manage and we would share the positive revenues on that shared split.

Without going into details, and under the circumstance we were in, it seemed we didn't have much of a choice. What happened next was a nightmare.

Within a week of our sending USIF's share of the rent proceeds, it was challenged. And a new war began.

My CFO and USIF accused each other of not adhering to the agreement and construction payments were being held up.

Meanwhile a Wall Street Journal article divulged financial problems with USIF alluding to it being a giant international "Ponzi scheme", which sent up a warning flag for us.

USIF purportedly had an office in Miami, so one of my close friends, California Senator John Briggs, volunteered to go with me to meet up with USIF at their office.

We flew to Miami only to discover the 'office' to be a mail drop facility. Now I was panicked—what had I gotten myself into?

Returning home, I was presented with another problem which I didn't need. The lady land owner with whom I entered into the land lease had died a few years earlier, and her estate was being managed by her daughter.

The daughter's lawyer boyfriend decided my sale of an interest in the project, had violated the land lease and sued for breach, attempting to take possession. I had no alternative but to get legal help.

The attorney that drew up the Brief against Belmont Savings had left Ball, Hunt & Brown and set up his own practice. He took the case on a contingency basis.

Meanwhile USIF was quickly collapsing in Europe and shock waves were moving westward to the U.S. It was scramble time.

I began selling my ancillary businesses; first, Bluebird Nursery to my partner, next Valencia Cleaners, then Huntington Harbor Liquors and last, Valencia Liquors. As the funds came in, I paid my contractors what they were owed and told them the future was in doubt for uncompleted contracts.

As USIF was going down in flames, my lawyer was ineffective in keeping us from losing everything, and we were forced into involuntary bankruptcy—my world had finally collapsed and I was financially finished.

So here I was, worth $3.5Million at age 40, Flat broke at age 41, definitely down, but not beaten.

***

Lesson Learned: In retrospect and using the 40-plus years of experience I have had since this bump in the road, I had way too many balls in the air at the same time. While each of my diverse businesses was profitable each took some of my attention away from my primary business, which was building and development.

I couldn't foresee the S & L doing what they did when they did it, but walking away and leaving them with the unfinished project would have been the smart thing to do.

I could have filed Bankruptcy on that project and left the S & L the problem, and protected all the other businesses by transferring ownership to a separate corporation—it's done all the time. Like they say, 'hind sight is always 20-20.

***

Blue Bird Nursery

Searching for my next project in Belmont Heights in Long Beach, we found a large lot that was suitable for 16-untis that was for sale currently being used as a commercial plant nursery; but this nursery had a unique kind of plant as its primary product. Commonly known as an Epiphyllum—a beautiful multiple petal Lily-like flower in a variety of shapes, a succulent grown in arid climates.

The owner was selling the property complete with all of the plants and wouldn't sell unless everything went—he was retiring.

We put the property in escrow after the owner accepted our offer, and began looking at options for disposing the plants. The owner gave me the name of a person who had a very large collection of the plants in Whittier CA north of us and a suburb city in the LA basin and former home of President Nixon.

We visited that person who did have a huge collection of the plants as an avid collector/grower. One thing led to another and the next thing I knew, I had a property for development of an apartment, an additional collection of Epiphyllums and a partner in a new business: "Blue Bird Nursery".

I was informed by my new partner/manager of our new business, that we now had the largest collection of Epiphyllum plants in the world, according to the "Southern California Epiphyllum Society", so I thought I had better do some research on the subject.

The lore of any given 'rare' item with any long term history unless found in authenticated publication can usually be taken with a grain of salt.

The story I was told by my new partner was that the plant was rare and favored by Adolph Hitler, who upon the breakout of the war, confiscated all known plants and forbade their propagation. There was no google at the time of our founding Blue bird Nursery, but I have since used Wikipedia as my source for this writing, which is probably the best of any source given the importance of including the information here.

According to Wikipedia: This species was shown at an exhibition at the Royal Horticultural Society's Garden in 1844 and won highest medal for a new introduction. It had been collected in **Honduras** five years earlier by **Georges Ule Skinner** and sent to Sir **Charles Lemon** who flowered it for the first time in 1843. **Lindley** thought it to have originated in the island of **Antigua**. E. crenatum is the only species of Epiphyllum that has been used in **hybridization** to any extent. Most of the colored hybrids have mainly Disocactus genes and perhaps better referred to as Disocactus-hybrids rather than Epiphyllum hybrids.

However, I did not find any reference to the story of Hitler's confiscation of the plants.

The plant is quite easily propagated from cuttings of its leaves, and being a succulent, those leaves are thick like certain cactus, but have no needles.

So my partner and I developed a plan to sell and propagate full plants locally, but adopt a mail-order program for selling the plants nationwide.

First, all of the plants were transported to a site located next to our commercial buildings in Rancho Valencia, and given show space facing the boulevard frontage. An appropriate sign was placed on the open-air structure with 'Plants for Sale' emblazoned below the logo for Blue Bird Nursery.

We designed small paper bags with the Bluebird Logo on them and readied our plan, when the bottom began to drop out of my world................

Bottom line, we were going to be out of business before we got started; I had to start fighting for my business life with everything I had at my disposal; My lender, Belmont Savings & Loan was in trouble, as were several other lenders as the real estate market began to soften.

There was no time to start a new venture. It was man the lifeboats time; every man for himself. I informed my new partner I was sorry but he was on his own and he could stay or leave at his choice rent free or move.

That was the short life of Blue Bird Nursery.

I turned all of my attention to the battle at hand; my fight for survival.

Next, we had to find a lender that would give us a construction loan on the ten duplexes so we could finish the entire project and move on. That took us to places geographically and financially that we weren't prepared for.

***

Bill Effinger

Huntington Harbor Liquors

A year after our liquor store opened, there was another ABC drawing, so naturally I posted another $6,500.00 and waited for the results. Unbelievably, my name was drawn again!

The location I had used for the possible store was an abandoned Shell gas station on Pacific Coast Highway (1) in Seal Beach, directly across from the entrance of the new Huntington Harbor Homes, a new subdivision of upscale Canal-facing homes. There was a Bank of America temporary facility on one side of that entrance, increasing daily traffic.

My plan for the existing building was to use it almost as it existed, which required some special approval from the ABC.

What I intended, was to gut the building of everything but the restroom facilities, install a cooler vault, fill the vacated space with the maximum fixtures space would allow, including a sales counter, and leave the two garage bay door pull-ups in place. There were no structures behind anything on our side of the Highway—it was sandy beach all the way to the ocean. Given our climate of continual sunshine and very little rain, I saw no problem—and it wasn't.

The pumps were already gone, but the tall pole with the Shell sign on top was still there. We pulled that down, had an equally large sign with a tilting blue Anchor adorning a white background declaring the name of our new business "Huntington Harbor Liquors."

My family and I were avid sailors at the time, competing in weekly local and extended races, as well as making frequent runs to Catalina Island on weekends and holidays.

The Huntington Harbor homes, facing the canals were ideally situated for another of my marketing schemes, delivery of the store's product right to the homes, via canal.

To do that I purchased a "Boston Whaler", powered it with a 50-horse Mercury outboard and we were in the liquor delivery business. Additionally, for the weekly "Wet Wednesday" racing season, we offered delivery to the docked boats in "Alamitos Bay Yacht Cub" and "Long Beach Yacht Club"—that also gave us a lot of attention and free publicity.

Confessions of a Serial Entrepreneur

Our gross sales were over the top and when it came time to sell the store, the price was indicative of the success we were having with our unique liquor store

***

Friends using Rum Runner following us as we finish a race

Lesson Learned: When ideas seem crazy to everyone you know and the people of experience in your field of endeavor caution you on the mistakes you are making, it's ok to stop and listen; but many times the probability of your success lays within those negative, cautionary and well-meaning Comments.

Examples abound of "You can't do that" being overcome as doubters look on in awe: Landing men on the moon, the I-Phone, the Internet—I could fill several pages with examples.

Dare to be different!

Valley View Appaloosa Ranch

Earlier, I mentioned our family was avid sailors; that is true with a small deviation: while my daughter, the youngest of our four and the only girl enjoyed sailing, she was an animal lover. While I was licking my wounds from the misadventure of what you have read in the chapter on Rancho Valencia, attempting to figure out our next move—other than moving from our beautiful recently constructed new home in Belmont Park, which we could no longer afford, our daughter mentioned she had always wanted a horse.

That dovetailed quite nicely with what I had decided to do—move to the country, far away from our ocean-adjacent home in Long Beach and start a new chapter. All I needed to do was find where.

My earliest adventure with boating was when I built my first boat, a 12-foot runabout that we christened in Lake Elsinore in 1952. Formed by rain runoff and no source other than rain, the lake was subject to drying up from time to time.

Very rural and separated by the Mountains from the Coast, Elsinore Valley situated in Riverside County was home to mostly hay farmers and horse ranchers and property values were relatively cheap.

So I put my land buying hat on and began a search for the right property. I had limited funds from consulting with contractors, which I immediately began doing after losing everything and I certainly wasn't going to get a loan quite yet, so the options were limited.

I settled on an odd triangular-shaped 31-acre parcel which up to this point, no one had been able to figure out what to do with in the small town of Wildomar, population less than two hundred fifty.

There was a school, a real estate office and a small convenience store and that was it.

Adding to the oddity of the site I chose, was that its southern property line (the longest in the triangle) was the boundary line of the town of Murrieta, slightly larger than Wildomar with a restaurant, bank, real estate office, farm supply and feed store and a grocery store, population around five hundred.

The asking price for the property was ten thousand dollars—less than $350 Dollars per acre—a true bargain, assuming I could make it useable. That was a third of what any other land in the area was selling for: obviously because of its shape and that it faced a sweeping "S-curve" in the road and the land rose from its base on the valley floor two-hundred feet to the top and tip of the triangle—the view was spectacular from there.

I made a cash offer and it was accepted. Our entire family spent weekends on the property building fences grading and shaping a road and getting ready for our move from the house we were renting in Newport Beach to a new rural—very rural life. Our two youngest children were still with us, daughter 12, and son 16.

Our new temporary home was an eight-foot by twenty-foot trailer, parked under a wood porte-cochere with an eight foot by twenty foot wooden porch, I built. The temperatures ranged from warm to very warm to hot.

For water, (we had yet to dig a well) my son and I would put a 50-gallon barrel in the back of the pickup truck (our only transportation) and drive to the school, where we would hook up our hose to an outside spigot and fill the barrel each day for bathing and cooking.

***

After moving into the trailer the first building we constructed was a small barn in which we stored some furnishing we had kept from our home in Long Beach. We would put them into a mobile home when I had enough money to purchase one.

I needed something more than a few consulting gigs to sustain us, so I approached the local Real Estate Broker/owner of Turner Real Estate, in Wildomar. The company had three active offices: one in Wildomar, one in Murrieta and one in the neighboring town of Temecula, destined to become the largest city in the valley.

Dave Turner, the broker of record and son of the founder, kept his office in Wildomar where he had his home. I introduced myself, explained my background and circumstances showed him my active real estate license and asked him if he had room for me. He said he would think about it and contact me—we had no phone as yet and of course cell phones hadn't yet been invented, so he would have to come to our—'Ranch'.

A few days later, Turner came up to our trailer, where I was working in the heat, hot, sweaty and dirty, grinding up the earth with a rented rototiller, getting ready to start a garden.

He looked at me, shook his head, smiled and said he couldn't believe that here I was, after being on top of the heap, so to speak, working like a Chicano laborer. We laughed at that and then he said he would give me a try.

All of his crew were local "Good Ole" Boys' mostly over their prime and pretty set in their ways—having a stranger in their midst from the "Big City" might be a problem, so Turner wanted to watch and listen for a while.

I took a couple of days touring all of Turner's listings to familiarize myself with what I would be attempting to sell, and then from the desk I had been assigned, began making calls.

Back at the ranch, I hired a well digger from Temecula who came highly recommended, and after water-witching the area, he picked a spot to start digging. After a few weeks and 250 feet later, which had seemed like an expensive eternity (we paid by the foot) , I was told the digger had struck an aquafer and we had a well that would produce 250 gallons per minute, which was like striking oil, because over the years the water table had been steadily receding.

Now that we had the kind of water needed to build a working ranch, our work began in earnest. My weekdays were mostly taken up in the real estate office, so weekends were devoted to the ranch projects.

***

My first few days in the office were spent working the Rolodex, calling former business associates, contractors, and yachting friends, telling them where I was what I was doing and explaining the area was ripe for growth and there were opportunities here.

A major company had recently purchased 2,500 acres, the largest ranch in the area, and begun developing "Rancho California" consisting of hundreds of smaller parcels ranging in size from the smallest: 1-acre to 20-acres, ostensibly to create Ranchetts for horse lovers.

Soon my phone calls began reaping benefits and I began showing and selling Turner-listed properties. I was happy, Turner was happy, but his crew grumbled—I was selling their listings, which of course they weren't. The simple fact was they knew all the property owners but had to wait for a client. I, of course, didn't know the property owners but I was generating clients through my contacts, of which there were many.

Back at the ranch, I kept my word with my daughter. We had kept one stall open in our little barn for when we found a horse, and we did. It was more a pony than a horse. She named it Sunshine and it was love at first sight.

My son and I began marking out pastures, laying irrigation lines and digging fence post holes to separate the area into several individual pastures—obviously I had bigger plans but they hadn't yet fully formulated in my mind.

After I made a very large sale on a property that had been listed for a couple of years and all of Turners crew to a man said it would never be sold, all hell broke loose. I had banked $80,000.00 in commissions in less than a year and it became a real problem for Turner.

My commissions were poured into our growing ranch as my vision for what it might become one day began to formulate into a plan to possibly join our valley neighbors as horse breeders.

Then I listed a very large property owned by the estate of the writer Earl Stanley Gardner located just outside the town of Temecula and adjacent to Rainbow, another small ranching town.

With that listing, Turner's crew got very restless and it looked like there was a mutiny in formation.

I targeted three potential buyers for the property: Raymond Burr, who had played Gardner's Perry Mason in the TV series, Ronald Reagan, who owned 600 acres in the mountains overlooking Temecula Valley, and my Former boss, Nathan Shapell, whom I had just seen a picture of on a horse, in a Palm Springs magazine.

I asked my Senator Friend John Briggs to see if he could put me in touch with Reagan or one of his people, and I called Nathan.

The property had three guest cabins, a main house with a full blown commercial kitchen—an ideal corporate retreat; but there was one feature that was incredible: one of the largest Oak trees I had ever seen was located just below all of the out buildings.

The main trunk was at least eight foot in diameter. Its lower branches were a foot thick leaving the main trunk pointing upward, then bending in an inverted U, dropping to the ground and then bending upward again, forming a tree-leaved canopy that would measure five-hundred square feet or more—what a place for a group seminar!

I never reached Reagan or Burr, but Nathan Shapell wanted to meet with me.

Ironically, shortly before I went to Beverly Hills to meet with my former boss, Dave Turner came to the ranch on a weekend where I was sweaty and hard at work doing some "ranching". He approached me in a hesitant manner and said: "Bill, this is really embarrassing, but I have a real revolt on my hands and my crew has said if you don't leave, they will."

I had seen this coming so I wasn't surprised.

He added: I can't believe I'm saying this but I have to ask you to quit coming to the office, before I lose my business. You have produced more in a year than all of them combined, but you are a big city guy and you won't be staying, so I have to do this; I am really sorry."

This was the first time I had ever been fired from a job, and it was for doing too much—amazing.

So we shook hands and that was it.

My visit with Nathan Shapell turned out a bit better

***

Confessions of a Serial Entrepreneur

Nathan greeted me cordially, and autographed the picture of him on a horse which he handed to me as I walked into his office. I was dressed in my ranch clothes, blue jeans, boots and a work shirt—all of my dress clothes were packed waiting for our mobile home to be purchased when I had the money to do so.

I told him about the Gardener property and why I thought he should consider buying it, but he had no interest.

Not being a person who wasted time, my old boss wanted me to return to the company. He was very aware of what had happened to me and my businesses, chastised me for not coming to him for help and then explained that he was losing control of his company since they had gone public and expanded beyond California.

No longer "S & S Construction Company"; the company was now "Shapell Industries Incorporated" a New York Stock Exchange traded company.

I told him that I would have to discuss his proposal to my wife and I would get back to him in a few days.

My wife was not happy. She was looking forward to completing the ranch and living life in the slow lane, not wanting me to get back into the whirlwind.

We talked the issue to death for a few days, and I convinced her that if we were ever going to build the ranch into what I thought it could be, and have the 'good life' again, I needed to make the kind of money I and the family had become used to.

I called and made an appointment to meet Nathan to discuss some issues of importance, those being a start date, salary, position, and a signing bonus, which I told him I would use to finance a trip for my wife and I to spend a week in Hawaii to help soften the blow for her on my returning to the company.

We met, worked out all of the issues I had and a few he had, one of which was the long drive from the ranch in Wildomar to the Beverly Hills headquarters every day, a distance of 98-miles one way. I assured him the distance would be no problem and we shook hands.

***

Confessions of a Serial Entrepreneur

Bill Effinger

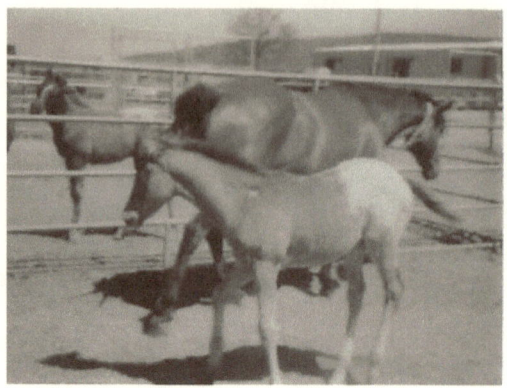

The above two pages include a story we published in our Western Appaloosa News about the legend of buried $20.00 Gold pieces somewhere on the ranch property by an early settler---we never found the treasure, but it made for good publicity about our ranch and the breeding operation.

1st Place~Valerie & 'Bucky'~LA County Fair~1978

Once we returned from Hawaii, and I was making the drive, Nathan began playing a game. His daily routine was to be in his office by 8:30 am, starting out with a toasted bagel and crisp bacon at

8:00am in the café on the ground floor of our office building on Wilshire Blvd. he expected everyone else to be there at 8:30am.

The game began with him setting an earlier time for us to meet in the café and share bagels and bacon. I was to meet him at 7:30. The next morning, I was there before he was. This went on until I was there ahead of him at the proposed 6:00 meeting and he laughed, shook his head and said "you win". Such was our relationship. What he didn't realize was that the earlier the meetings were set, the faster I could get there because the traffic was lighter.

***

My Ten Years with Shapell Industries

After joining Shapell Industries in 1971, I became Executive Vice President with responsibilities which included oversight of our subsidiaries in Northern California, Simi Valley, Colorado and San Diego. All Los Angeles, Long Beach, Orange and Riverside County projects were directed from Shapell headquarters in Beverly Hills. My role with those projects was as an observer only, reporting directly to the Chairman, Nathan Shapell.

Soon after, the San Diego subsidiary was becoming a problem with customer complaints generating negative publicity in the local papers. This was out of character for Shapell which had been building a reputation for quality homes and repeat home sales for many years.

Things got so bad that Nathan was considering shutting the operation down, so he asked me to go down there, nose around to see if the operation could be salvaged and report back.

After spending a week in San Diego talking to builders, realtors, bankers, S & L execs, and city officials I was convinced we should stay. I was also convinced that the subsidiary had some serious problems.

After carrying the message back to Nathan that we should stay, he said if we were going to keep operating in San Diego, I would have to go there and run the operation, but I would also have to keep my responsibilities with the Executive VP position.

So instead of driving 96 miles from the ranch to Beverly Hills, I would now be driving only 66 miles with much less traffic, although a two-lane road in those days.

I quickly fired everyone in the San Diego operation with the exception of the accounts payable person, a retired female naval officer, and retained a project manager who seemed to be worth salvaging. Then I began hiring a new crew, starting with the receptionist.

Over time, our division, Shapell Industries of San Diego, became the most profitable of all of our subsidiaries while building hundreds of homes and commercial structures throughout the county.

Bill Effinger

Encinitas Estates & Camino Park Encinitas

Camino Park North Encinitas

Monarch Hill & Monarch Place La Costa

Mission Ridge Mission Valley

Bill Effinger

Mission Greens Mission Valley SD

Presidio Place Mission Valley

Carmel Mountain Ranch I-15 Corridors SD

Experiencing a case of 'Mid-life Crisis' in 1980, my wife and I divorced after 32-years. I deeded the Valley View Ranch property, the breeding business and all of the livestock to her and moved out of our home. I also informed Nathan Shapell of my intent to leave the company.

Not wanting to accept my resignation, the company sent me on an all-expenses-paid European and Mediterranean trip. But the further I got away from San Diego, the more I knew I wanted to leave the company and do something I had been thinking about for a long time.

At the chairman's direction, all of our homes continued to get larger in square footage and added amenities. As a result, they became more expensive, leaving behind what I had felt was our founding premise of building homes for new home buyers as we were doing for returning veterans in the 50's.

I wanted to build houses for new home buyers but couldn't get Nathan to agree. My plan was to do it on my own.

***

Lesson Learned: When someone throws you a lifeline, grab it and hold on...there is no shame in allowing someone to come to your rescue when your boat is sinking. Next time, you may be the person throwing the lifeline. What goes around comes around in this life. And remember, there is no failure, just lessons learned for the next venture.

***

New Dimensions for Living, Inc.

After leaving Shapell, I rented a small office space in downtown San Diego to catch my breath and cast about for opportunities while visiting bankers and S & L's, testing the waters for possible funding for my planned venture.

My leaving Shapell was news in the industry because we had been a big part of the development scene in the county with all of our high-profile projects and the part we were playing in the local economy.

I had become somewhat of a business celebrity from all of this, so there were headlines in the business section of the local papers on my departure.

Soon after settling into my new office, I was contacted by someone I had never met nor heard from, asking to meet and discuss my representing him and his partner on an issue they had with the county. I agreed and we set a time and date.

When we met, the two men explained they had been trying to promote a second border crossing in Chula Vista and they couldn't get anywhere with the county. My representation for getting approvals on projects was well known and these men had noticed.

I agreed to take the assignment, agreed on a fee, and in a very short time managed to get the County's approval for the location they were seeking—my first and successful consulting assignment with a nice paycheck. Life was good.

I opened a business banking account in the bank situated on the ground floor of our building and introduced myself to the manager, told him I was a licensed real estate broker, and if he or any of his clients had a need, I was interested in helping.

Miraculously in that conversation, the banker said they were looking for a location in East San Diego and if I knew of one, he would pay me a commission—that resulted in my getting a $50K commission within three-weeks of his request. He was happy, I was ecstatic.

However, my main goal was to form a new company for the purpose of building for first time buyers, so I did. I filed incorporation papers for "New Dimensions for Living, Inc." its stated purpose was to build affordable housing.

The first thing I needed was someone who would help me design my product, was inexpensive, and would follow my directions with a minimum need for authorship; that wouldn't be an Architect, it would most likely be an Architectural draftsman with talent and a need for work.

Fortunately, I found him and we began working together on my dream product.

***

My newly found draftsman had a small studio in the Hillcrest area of San Diego where I began spending a great deal of my time as we jointly worked on what I wanted to do in developing a product that would sell and could be replicated on a broad scale in many communities.

Research that I personally conducted, indicated that much like Long Beach California, where I started my first venture in building within the infill areas, was quite typical to most cities which were planned when subdivisions were becoming widespread in the early thirties.

Lots were laid out in grid patterns of blocks, twelve blocks to a mile, fifty to sixty foot wide streets, each lot being fifty foot wide by one hundred feet deep to a twenty-five foot alley in the rear.

My plan was to create a multi density structure that would fit on those lots and would provide parking for one car per apartment unit.

When I began this venture in 1981, the bottom had fallen out of the real estate market and there were many unsold houses. More important, the market I intended to address was one that was yet to be tapped, in my view.

That market was the single, employed man or woman, working in the central part of the city that enjoyed the ambience and social structure of city life and wanted to live close to all the activity. There was a second market peculiar to where I was going to purchase my first lots—a college was in close proximity.

This opened up the possibility of selling units to parents of young people going to college where their student could live and/or share a unit and when they graduated, the unit would remain as an investment for either the student or the parents..

Another important element in the design was the density had to be adjustable to be able to alter the building design to accommodate a higher or lower density without altering the footprint. One of the things I learned in building and selling condominium buildings was that once you locked into individual apartment types, you were stuck with the unit yield of the design. When a project of single homes is being built and you realize you should have more of one type than another—you just make the adjustment. Not so with a multi-story multi-unit structure.

To address that problem, we designed our units to be adjustable upward or downward from 32 units to 52 units depending on the ratio number of studios, one and two bedroom units on the standard lot configurations outlined above. Our base building footprint required two adjacent lots of 50 foot by 100 feet to an alley of 20 to 25 feet.

***

Once the plans were completed, I started looking for construction loans, soon finding out that takeout financing was a must before I could get the construction loans, and that was going to be difficult. Unfortunately, there were no affordable housing agencies in existence at the time, so conventional sources were all that was available.

The search took a long time and many sales pitches to skeptical potential lenders before finding an S & L based in Phoenix Arizona, through a friend that was willing to give me the loan. But that was only after I had secured a firm commitment for the construction loan which two banks agreed to do a "piggy-back loan" (each bank sharing the risk).

My small staff created a Brass plaque with 14 tabs hanging from it, naming each of the turn-down banks which was laughingly presented to me and then hung prominently in the reception area of our little office.

Bill Effinger

After financing was secured, construction began on two pilot projects on sites I had acquired; one in the "Golden Hill" area of San Diego's historic, one-time Victorian mansions of the elite, also referred to as "Bankers Hill", ironic because it was so difficult for me to find a bank willing to loan me construction funds. The other site was in the "Hillcrest" area which was experiencing somewhat of a renaissance.

The architectural style we chose for the exterior of our building was designed to blend into the Victorian motif of the neighborhood rather than the pink stucco tile roofs so common throughout San Diego and Southern California as a whole. The result was that many drive-by observers thought our project was a remodel rather than new construction.

Applying my ability to churn publicity, there were numerous articles covering our experiment, which caught the eye of a building materials manufacturer in New England, and I was invited to speak to a large group of similar companies who held periodic group meetings to discuss trends in housing. The result was my being invited to attend their next meeting which was being held in the company town of Kohler Wisconsin, and explain my concept and the need for producing affordable housing.

The talk was well received which led to another invitation to speak to professors of Harvard, MIT, and "Fellows of Third World Countries" in a session being hosted in Boston.

The outgrowth of the presentation led to what appeared to be an opportunity of a lifetime.

***

The chairman of the board of one of the oldest building materials companies in the United States, Bird Roofing, Inc. (founded in 1795), reached out to me to set up a meeting to go into detail on my concept, plans for growth and the possibility of his company getting involved, perhaps even acquiring our company.

That was a big WOW for me at that time as one might imagine, and I eagerly accepted the invitation.

Meetings were set for me with various corporate people, to whom I explained our plan and how it would fit in a nationwide effort to build our products in numerous infill communities.

Following those meetings, I had a final meeting with the chairman in which he said the company would issue a 'letter of Intent to Acquire' after his accountants reviewed our books, project cost/profit analysis.

During the interim, I was to develop a business plan that would provide a scheme for rollout and staffing of the company. My head was buzzing and I was ecstatic.

Bird's management people arrived a week later and began their review of our numbers as I developed the requested plan.

Part of my original plan before Bird entered the scene was to introduce my product in a unique way: one of our planned units was a Studio of 360 square feet, and the first building to be constructed was to be located on two contiguous lots in "Golden Hill", a few short blocks from the center of the downtown San Diego business district.

Fortuitously, a corner storefront on 7th and Broadway, downtown's main street was available for lease. I leased the space and built an exact replica of the studio, in the space and set up a section outside of the mockup studio as a sales room.

We had a lighted storefront sign displayed in large letters: "Condominiums From the $30,000's".

Opening day of the sales office/model was on "Tax Day, April 15th 1982".

From noon to closing, "Fro Brigham & His New Orleans Jazz Band" was on the sidewalk in front of the store playing Jazz & Blues to an amazed and ever growing crowd.

With help from the Mayor's office, I had arranged for Lieutenant Governor Mike Curb to view the model and as a result, the media was in full force.

As mentioned above, things were fairly slow in new home sales.

The market was declining due to rising costs—so response to our numbers were hard to believe which caught the imagination of my intended market, the young professional.

Our opening day was a show stopper—we took 128 reservations for the yet-to-be constructed units in the first week. Considering our Golden Hill building was only going to have 111 units, we took deposits on our second scheduled building in Hillcrest which would have 108 units.

The chairman of Bird and his people were duly impressed and construction began in earnest.

The "Pacific Coast Builders Conference" was scheduled for June of 1982, so we booked a booth space and prepared a demonstration of the uniqueness of our flexible design, using a large table type board. The board was cut to match the outside dimensions of a standard building.

Each of our studio, one and two-bedroom unit floorplans were cut out in plastic shapes cut to scale matching the floor plans like jig saw puzzle pieces, each were different colors.

My oldest son Kirk was working for our company at the time and he became so proficient at maneuvering the unit/pieces around the building outline, that on the convention floor, he would gather a mesmerized crowd of builders, bankers and looky-loos.

To my delight, the San Francisco Examiner gave us a two-page spread in the business section of the paper that weekend—we were on a roll.

※※※

Our Store Front Model, 7th & Broadway, San Diego

Studio Model 'A' 340 sq. ft. $29,900 with wall bed extended

Studio Model 'A' shown with bed Retracted

Following the PCBC experience, the Chairman of Bird, asked to have a meeting with me and all of my staff in San Diego to discuss out future plans.

Our crew and the chairman met for breakfast at the popular "Bahia Resort", spending a few hours getting acquainted and discussing the potential for our two companies when the potential merger/acquisition was to take place.

The Chairman had asked me to arrange a Golf game for him on the popular "Mission Valley Stardust Country Club" golf course. I wasn't a golfer at the time, so I asked my very close friend Herb Seltzer if he wouldn't mind doing the honors and he gracefully obliged.

Before leaving San Diego, the Chairman and I arranged what was to be the final meeting at Bird's main campus in Walpole, whereupon I was ostensibly to pick up a very large check to begin the launch of our new venture.

※※※

Arriving at the appointed time after a long Red-eye from San Diego, I was shown to a waiting room, where I was told there was a board meeting in progress that was taking longer than expected and the chairman offered his apologies for the delay.

A little more than two-hours later, one of the Bird staff members who had been part of the team examining our books and business plan came up to me with a grim look on his face and simply said "the deal is off".

My heart began racing as a million thoughts rolled through my mind, none of them good. I asked to speak to the chairman and I was told he did not want to meet with me--so much for a "Letter of Intent" and handshakes and golf games. Lesson learned the hard way.

After the Bird debacle, we completed and sold both buildings, but financing had completely dried up, so we shut down our operation, chalking up the experience as a very bad one which we vowed would never happen to us again.

Lesson Learned: Corporations are not "people" as our current Supreme Court has ruled in the "Citizens United" case for campaign finance.

A corporation has no conscience, nor honor. A corporation is a vehicle for people to hide behind with a shrug of their shoulders and a "that's business" comment.

I learned the hard way that a 'letter of intent' is just that a statement that one party intends to (but is not obligated to) do whatever the two parties have discussed.

Seek legal advice when dealing with any corporation no matter how large or small, or how long they have been in business.

***

Techno Data, Inc. Developed Construction Software

Around the time of the Bird debacle, desk top computers and the software programs that made them into more than typewriters and calculators was becoming the big thing; but the construction industry was slow to react. Wood and nails, hammers and saws they related to, but high-tech wasn't yet seen as being applicable to this traditionally "come up from the field, constructing buildings" as has been done for eons.

Having had the experience of helping run a major public building company and some of the cost tracking issues we had, I sensed a need. Seeing a possible opportunity and the need to once again lick my wounds from a bad experience, I decided to pursue that opportunity.

This led to my next business adventure: I set out to create a software program exclusively for the construction industry.

The formation of the idea to develop a software program for the construction industry, developed out of my and Shapell Industries Chairman, Nathan Shapell's frustration with how untimely the normal accounting process was in tracking our costs.

Our company was averaging 400 housing units being completed every month. Granted, this is way above the average building company, but it accentuated the problem.

Closings on sales were at the same clip; so when you received your cost sheets, the reports reflected where you were when the books were closed on the 15th of last month and it was the thirtieth of this month, in our case, 45-days. We were closing sales on 600 houses before we knew what their cost was. Not good!

I was convinced the failure of many small builders and contractors could be pointed to that problem. While at Shapell, I devised a complicated, hand written cost-to-profit tracking system that we insisted the accounting departments of our subsidiaries and our home office adopt, so we could have better, up to the minute figures.

My idea was to duplicate that system with the software I was planning on creating. All I needed was a software program writer to transfer my system to computer code. That proved to be more difficult than I had expected; but with some help, I eventually got it done.

I had been guest lecturing for a professor friend of mine at San Diego's National University. His classes were for BA and MBA students, and my usual topic was on entrepreneurism. The university had an active computer engineering program, part of which was Programing. My friend suggested a couple of whizzes the professor of the Programing class recommended, so I met with them, explained what I wanted to do and they started to write the program.

That didn't work out unfortunately. The two young men could really write code; but they couldn't convert their codes to the English language—in short, they didn't understand where I wanted to go with the equations I needed them to write their algorithms, and I couldn't understand their algorithms when they created them—so we parted company.

***

Next, I visited a new IBM store that recently opened selling their new desktop PC's and on a hunch, asked the manager if he might know someone who understood code writing, explaining to him what I wanted to do.

Fortunately, the manager had a name for me of someone he had recently talked to who was a recently retired Navy Chief with hardware and software experience who was looking for something to do. I called the number and set up an appointment to meet the person in Coronado where he lived with his wife.

We met in a small coffee shop and immediately hit it off. I had been stationed on Coronado's Naval Air Station in 1947 and 48' when I was in the Navy, so we went from there. I will only use his first name here to protect his privacy: Since that first meeting, Frank became one of my closest and most admired friends.

Extremely well read in many topics, calm in demeanor with a great sense of humor, Frank was a great balance for my impetuous, quick to react temperament as we began the development and marketing of the software. He loved my Socratic method of questioning things and we spent hours discussing a broad range of topics over the next several years.

We had important work to do, so I set up a table in my second floor apartment's living room which overlooked the swimming pool—I was unmarried at the time and we both enjoyed the view of the ladies in their swim suits as a welcome break from the tedium of creating code for the software.

What my program was designed to do, was create a spread sheet that covered every line item in the building of a structure, down to the smallest element that had a cost and every contractor or supplier involved in the finished product. Including construction loan cost, overhead and sales costs.

Every time there was a change, that change would calculate the final cost carried out to the established sales price, alerting the builder to the cost change and the need to increase the cost and ultimate sales price of the product—simple. But complex, requiring multi-dimensional calculations that Lotus 123 creators were not aware their program could do—the result was they featured us in their monthly Magazine as a WOW!

I needed a name for the enterprise, so I chose: "Techno Data, Inc.". I filed corporation papers for my company with California's "Corporations Commissioner", but hadn't yet come up with a suitable name for the product. That came later.

When we had a prototype finished that would do what I wanted it do, we needed to test it to see if anyone in the construction industry would want to acquire the product. I paid a visit to the IBM store manager who had introduced me to Frank, and asked if he had space and time in his demo room to allow us to show off our product. He said yes, as he saw the opportunity to possibly sell his PC's to the attendees.

The date was set, and he put the word out in the local paper, plus a couple flyers. By this time, I picked the unimpressive name for the product as "Construction Cost Software" that soon changed.

**

The attendance was beyond what I had hoped for on the evening we had picked. Demo room packed with interested builders and contractors, I began putting the program through its paces. I interject here the fact that Frank had decided that the quickest and easiest way to accomplish what I was after with the program was to use the new Lotus 123 spreadsheet program to dove tail ours with it, as our needs were partially met with the Lotus base. That proved to be the best and worst decision over time, but I will explain that later.

The showing was a success, and along with several potential purchasers, a gentleman who had been watching intently, came up to me after the demonstration, introduced himself as a manager of a "Cubic Corporation" subsidiary charged with finding new products and asked for a meeting.

Cubic was a company founded locally, which produced a wide variety of products, most under government contract.

The Cubic manager and I met a few days later, and an arrangement was made wherein the Cubic subsidiary would bankroll a refinement of the product and a marketing rollout with an $80,000.00 infusion of capital; but there was one hitch—we had to adapt our program to function with a Wang computer.

This man from Cubic was convinced that Wang was going to be the future of PC"s which both Frank and I found contra to everything we were seeing and experiencing up to now, but why turn down $80,000.00? Particularly when two Wang computers were part of the deal we made.

As fast as we worked on the new software to adapt to Wang, it became increasingly evident that Wang was on the way out. The result was the Cubic Subsidiary man lost interest and we parted ways.

Lesson learned: when a partnership isn't working and it interferes with the basic business plan, cut the losses and move on. As my grandmother used to say "you can't make a silk purse out of s sow's ear." And in our view, Wang was on its way to becoming extinct.

Builders Construction Software: Marketed Software

Using what funds I had retained from the Cubic deal, I rented a small space in Old Town San Diego (I don't remember why), set up shop as 'Techno Data, Builder's Construction Software' and began meeting with contractors and builders and selling the product, making enough to keep the doors open, but not setting the world on fire.

***

A couple of months later and out of the blue, the Chairman of Bird, whom I will now identify as 'George', the man who had sold me down the river with my New Dimensions for Living building program, contacted me, saying he would buy me a round trip ticket to Boston and a few nights in a hotel, if I would come there to meet with some people in his organization who were working on something related to computers and going nowhere. He also said he had heard through the grapevine about my software.

Always subscribing to the theory that when opportunity knocks you better listen, I agreed. Flights were arranged and a week later I found myself in Boston. The following day, I was on the Bird Campus in Walpole, an hour's drive on a good day, from Boston.

Meeting with the Bird chairman and his people, it was clear that what they were working on was a marketing plan for selling roofing to roofing contractors, using Apple Computer's graphics and the internet, which was in its infancy, AOL being the predominant player.

I was then asked to talk about my software, explain how it would be used by all contractors and builders, which was a much broader market than what they were planning to reach. A fairly lengthy discussion ensued, after which I was thanked for my time and told by George he would be in touch.

I returned to San Diego the next day.

***

Confessions of a Serial Entrepreneur

About a week later, George called and said he was sending me another plane ticket, and that I should come back with the intention of entering into an agreement where bird would acquire the rights to my program, and I would be engaged as the marketer/chairman of a Bird subsidiary we would identify as 'Bird Construction Software'. To cinch the deal, I would be given options for Bird stock and a salary we would negotiate. This sounded like it might be worth pursuing so I agreed to come back to Boston.

***

My life immediately went from scraping a meager living selling the software and a few consulting assignments, to what had the potential of making it big in the software world.

This time, before making any kind of move, I got assurances, the stock option and salary agreement up front, along with a signed agreement to move all of my home furnishings and car when I had found an apartment to live in while I was there. Meanwhile I commuted from San Diego to Boston, staying in a hotel when there.

About six weeks into commuting, I found what for me, was the perfect apartment for the move. An apartment on famous "Beacon Street", a half block from where they were filming the popular TV series, "Cheers" in the basement level of a small hotel, where above, I would be having Sunday Breakfast in their quaint restaurant.

The first floor apartment of four levels was formerly one of the "Boston Brahman's" mansions constructed in 1853, twelve years before Lincoln's assassination became my new home.

Directly across the street, was the world famous "Public Gardens" with its "Swan Boats" and thousands of Tulips every spring. Needless to say, history buff that I am, I was ecstatic at the find.

Returning to San Diego, I engaged a moving company to pack and load everything I owned including my Honda Accord, and then returned to Boston to begin the adventure.

Lessons learned: While keeping your head down and plowing forward in your venture, don't forget to look up and take a long

look at your competition and the changes that are probably occurring in the industry you are involved with.

In my case, the leap from a world comparatively slow moving hammer and nails, boards and concrete, to a digital world that was on its way to establishing 'Moore's Law' where everything doubles itself every two years, became a prophetic experience as I partnered with a 200-year old company.

***

Bird Construction Software Inc. Licensed Techno Data and Builders Construction Software

While I was getting ready to move to Boston on the long commute, I did a great deal of reading on selling products using telemarketing and it intrigued me. I did some research and found one of the biggest telemarketing companies in the U.S., was located in Provo Utah, originally founded by the Mormons to sell bibles with their version of Christian History. The name of the company was "The Nice Corporation" of course it was.

After making contact with them I booked a flight to Salt Lake where I rented a car, drove to Provo and met with the manager of the "Nice" operation, which was mind boggling huge. The building was massive and crowded with hundreds of small booths, each with a phone, head phones and monitor and an equal number of Telemarketers manning the booths—I was blown away.

The manager explained all of the nuances of his operation and the importance of picking the right people for the job. My marathon reading of the books on the subject were right on with what they had said about picking the right people, not good "sellers", but good "listeners"; preferably part time rather than full time, because of the grueling monotony and the high rate of rejection.

I told him what I had in mind: every company that was producing software was sending sample discs to their target market, including AOL who was actually sending you ready access to the internet—FREE!

In my mind, that was a cost that would be a burden to our startup, so I devised a plan of selling our discs for the magic "tele-selling" number of $19.95 including shipping & handling—that would be a perceived bonus from the usual TV message of the product hustlers.

We negotiated and arranged a test of five days making outbound calls to our target market—small builders and contractors throughout the country. We would offer a discount price on the purchase of the product if they purchased the demo disc.

The plan was to develop a matrix of the number of calls it would take to get to a decision maker, how many decision makers would purchase a disc, and the number of disc sales it would take to sell a full program.

Obviously a five day test would not sell final product but using the Nice Company statistics, we could get a workable number which we could set as a goal.

I no longer have the matrix figures, but when we started our telemarketing effort, the ratio of calls, to disc sales to conversions to full programs was eerily close to what we were told it would be by the "Nice" people. The next step was to hire a crew of telemarketers. We had a full crew of part-timers within thirty days.

Developing a marketing plan on a nationwide scale for our product was the next order of business. Bird had its own in-house advertising and graphic design department, which George put at my disposal, so we went to work immediately to design the packaging.

I chose a color design with the patriotic colors of red, white and blue, figuring I would use the history of Bird, formed shortly after the revolutionary war and the signing of the American Constitution.

Our full product line once we were up and running

We needed to build a small marketing team, so the employee who had been working on the Bird software that wasn't going anywhere was assigned to me and I hired a young recent college graduate with a degree in marketing and economics to help me search for a couple of others to add to the team.

We were given a building on the Bird main campus that had housed a grounds keeper at one time. The Bird campus housed a large group of manufacturing buildings, but their headquarters were located off-campus, much to our delight, because we were truly a "skunk works" operation.

Bird Construction Software Headquarters

Following the Nice company manager's suggestion of looking for Teachers who needed part time work, they were trained listeners. That's what we did and the manager was right, the two teachers we had found, outdid the other callers by a large margin.

Not only did they prove to be excellent, but also attractive

We began making calls, selling discs and making appointments within a week of working up the scripts, as two of our people were searching numbers of building and construction companies to call.

While the team was making calls, we began getting ready for the upcoming "National Association of Home Builders" (NAHB) Convention in Dallas. We wanted to have a booth that would house a hands-on demonstration that could be used by a visitor to push a few keys using some of his own cost records so he/she could watch the results of the calculations appear on the computer screen.

To do that I designed a three-foot square by eight-foot tall upright box of plywood with a chest-high cutout with a shelf that would support a desktop computer and monitor. The box was topped with a gabled roof adorned with Bird Shingles—their primary product, and of course painted red, white and blue.

Later, we liked the results from the show, so we planned to get permission to place the units in various building material and hardware supply stores where contractors frequented, using Bird's relationships to convince the supply-house owners. Unfortunately I no longer have a picture of this unit.

Our Tele-Team followed up on the hundreds of leads we received on the show floor, scoring quite well with several full program sales. Below is a picture of one of the phone cubicles our team spent their four hour days in with hourly breaks.

One of the eight tele-booths in our office

Following that, we received permission to put on a Seminar for the "Greater Boston Home Builders Association" for a demonstration, out of which came the idea to create a class for small contractors.

The response was overwhelming, so we decided to try booking similar seminars in other cities and states. To accomplish that, we brought on two tech-savvy salesmen to conduct the product seminars.

When our operation was first funded, Bird only put their toes in the water agreeing to a startup budget of six months. I wasn't comfortable with this, having to hire several people that could only last for such a short time, so when I interviewed them, I explained this was all experimental and could end abruptly—I wasn't going to lie to them. That tactic worked to instill loyalty among my team members.

That arrangement continued for two years until we realized the world was passing us by. Bird refused to allow a ramp up of our efforts of redesigning our product by funding an updated version of the software, which we realized was rapidly becoming overshadowed by the new startup Microsoft and those forward looking software engineers who recognized its power.

But when your partner is a 200-year-old company that manufactures shingles, and has allowed their company to slip from dominance of its products to almost going out of business, it doesn't seem to fit with staying up to the fast moving digital world which was moving at never before experienced speeds.

The result was that after two-years of living with this every six month funding and realizing we were losing ground, I asked to meet with the board of directors over the objections of Chairman George, asking them to pull the plug and release my licensing agreement; which they did.

Within a few weeks, I formed a new company, located and rented a small office, hired a tech writer to help write the manual for my product which I redesigned the packaging and with Frank's help update our software, breaking it into three parts thereby allowing the purchase of individual elements that could be used by a contractor without having to purchase the entire package, which of course lowered the purchase price, but we were still being out-distanced and the handwriting was on the wall.

We named the new product "The Competitive Edge".

***

As stated earlier, what goes around comes around, and in this case, I was able to be handsomely paid for experimenting with an idea I was allowed to pursue for a period of slightly over two-years by the same company that had basically helped to put me out of business two-years earlier.

I viewed this as a pay-back proffered by the Chairman of Bird Corporation for having done what he had, without an apology—turnabout is fair play as they say.

Builders Marketing & Management Services, Inc.

After we shut down the Bird operation, Bird released the licensing agreement we had negotiated with them, allowing me to pursue the repackaging of the product, renamed the "The Competitive Edge" and designed a new presentation for it.

My intent was to launch a consulting business, using my software as part of what I would be helping my contractor and builder clients turn their business around to being profitable.

I spent a few months developing a comprehensive Syllabus for a series of 12 classes to be given over the same number of weeks, which we titled "Survive Succeed and Grow in the Building and Contracting Business".

The Greater Boston Builders Association sponsored the program which we held in their facility, and we split the tuition 50/50 which was $450 per student/contractor.

The attendance was the first surprise—40 contractors representing a broad class of trades, as well as a few builders and general contractors, both residential and commercial.

Each attendee was given a homework assignment which would be reviewed and commented on by the group and they would be graded on their presentation. We set a competitive goal for the class with incentive: the person with the highest grade at the end of the 12 sessions would have the entire class fee refunded; the second best would get a 50% refunded and the third highest would receive a 25% refund.

In reality every member of the class was a winner, because each of them had a completed business plan and marketing plan for their respective business, which is what the course was promised to deliver and the plan had been critiqued by their peers.

Awards and grades were handed out on a fun "Graduation Evening".

We recorded every class on video in order to be able to make changes in what we felt would make the classes better for the future. Every class had a guest lecturer who had experience in the topic of the evening.

The class was a roaring success and drew comments in the "Boston Business Journal" and the "Boston Globe". I quickly became a regular contributor to the Business Journal, which helped with acquiring clients and selling the software. I also became a contributor to "Builder Magazine" a NAHB monthly publication distributed nationally, and "NAHB Builders' Journal".

The publicity paid off in many ways helping to promote my consulting business and sale of the Competitive Edge product on a national scale. I soon became restless to return to San Diego, my California home of many years, and so many business and political associates I had built up over the years.

***

I had purchased a ¾ ton Ford dually to haul a 32-foot fifth-wheel that I planned to tour the country with, which sat idly parked behind our Bird office building for over a year, neither ever having been on the road.

I missed my family, all on the west coast, and the chances for consulting assignments were much better where I knew many more people in the industry and political circles, so I began making plans to move back to California.

I gave notice to my landlords of the Beacon Street Apartment and my office space and was soon on the road with my never used truck, hauling the never used fifth wheel across the wide expanse of America.

***

Bill Effinger

Mr. Effinger
Chairman
Bird Construction
Software

BILL EFFINGER'S Builders Marketing Trends

Cont. from the April 28, 1989 Builders Edition.

Why then, I wonder, are there so few builders and contractors using computers to improve their business?

Just what is everyone waiting for?

My guess is that a) most contractors and builders haven't yet organized their business in a logical enough order to put the information into a disciplined program; b) they are too busy putting out fires (I think the construction industry invented crisis management); c) they tell themselves they can't afford it; d) they talk themselves into thinking they will not need to automate until their competitor does; d) and when they do go looking for a hardware and software program their expectations are such that they think the computer will organize and operate all by itself. When it won't, they say, "See, I knew I didn't need one." "It won't do what I want it to do!"

Maybe all you need is some information to help you decide whether to automate or not. What follows is what I think are very good reasons to bring the computer into your business.

What a computer will not do:

1. It will not operate by itself.
2. It will not "organize" your business.
3. It will not plan, think, or design by itself.
4. It will not take the place of a secretary or bookkeeper if you currently have one or both.
5. And it will not "make you money" by itself.

Here is what a computer with the right software can do when it's properly installed and implemented:

1. It will accurately store, produce and reproduce all of your financial records — accounts receivable, general ledger, accounts payable and payroll. It will do job costing on individual projects and print out all of your checks. It will always be in "audit" condition for anyone to view.
2. It will help you plan and schedule your jobs, track progress monitor percentage of completion, control retention payments and keep accurate, traceable records in case of time delay disputes — time and material billings, etc....
3. It will make the estimating processes quicker and more accurate, thereby increasing the number of jobs you can estimate in a given period — which, of course, should increase the number of jobs you get.
4. It will analyze your bids and your competitors bids to help you be more competitive without giving up any of the anticipated profits.
5. With your input it can draw, re-draw, produce, store and print complete drawings in plan, perspective and section.
6. The computer can produce large numbers of "original" letters to prospects and clients with individualized addresses and salutations in a fraction of the time it would take someone to type them.
7. It can store a file of prospects and customers ready for instant viewing with an infinite amount of market profile information at your disposal.
8. A desktop computer can replace several large file cabinets full of business information.

As we approach the expect downturn in the national economy — and we all know that the construction industry is a major element in our economy — wouldn't it be wise to try and refine your day-to-day operations, your bidding procedures, job management and financial forecasting methods so you can be ready for the tighter competition for fewer and fewer projects? The answer, of course, should be a resounding YES!

Why not take advantage of these marvelous new tools being offered that help do all the necessary things we need to improve our management and efficiency?

The longer you wait the farther behind you will be. Wouldn't it be nice if the next time you need current financial information on your company and projected revenue far into the future that you could produce complete schedules and reports all "typed" and bound for your banker within minutes from the time they were requested?

There may be many valid reasons why we still build our projects in time tested ways. But I know of no valid reason why the smallest of modern businesses should not be using computers to assist in meeting the challenges of today.

Our industry is facing its largest challenge ever — to provide housing for first and last time buyers that is within the reasonable reach of their income, while land, labor and material prices are skyrocketing. One of the quickest routes to ensuring affordable pricing, is better, tighter design and better cost controls coupled with good money management skills and techniques. The computer offers an opportunity to those who will require a more efficient business environment to compete and provide affordable housing.

William Effinger, chairman, Bird Software, Walpole, Mass.

This article was taken from the New England Real Estate Journal Builders Edition, Friday, May 26, 1989.

Confessions of a Serial Entrepreneur

NATION'S BUILDING NEWS

THE NATIONAL ASSOCIATION OF HOME BUILDERS
THE VOICE OF AMERICA'S HOUSING INDUSTRY

MAY 23, 1988
VOLUME 4, NUMBER 8

Many Big Choices Are Involved in 'Computerization'

William R. Effinger

When to computerize and what part of your business to automate first.

Much has been written on this subject, but most of what one reads seems to come from the software vendor's point of view without ample consideration for the person whose business is going to be affected.

The first programs to be introduced to the building and remodeling industries were accounting programs. At last count there exist over 350 different accounting programs being sold as "construction accounting" programs. As a result of this proliferation of accounting oriented programs, the effort has been to convince the builder, general contractor or sub-contractor and remodeler that the first program one should install when computerizing should be accounting. The process appears to reflect the need of the vendor to sell rather than the contractor to "need" a given product.

Estimating now is being offered to the industry as well as CAD (computer aided design) and scheduling and enhancement tools. With these choices you can begin to select the program that best suits your needs when you first consider installing a computer. With these available choices you can intelligently focus on that portion of your business on which you spend the most time and is seemingly least productive. Automating to save time and become more accurate is what improves bottom line performance and makes the decision to computerize viable for your business.

When you are considering the investment of your money and time to install a computer, there is no need to automate your accounting first if you are getting good reports, know your costs and can keep your banker happy with your statements.

The questions you should ask yourself and those working with you are: What part of your business causes you the most trouble? Is it scheduling? Subs and material delivery? Planning the project? Are your designs professional looking? Are production schedules not being met? Estimates not accurate or timely in the completion? Are you pleased with the performance of your crews? Is it easy keeping track of your customers, past and present? Can you be consistent in your follow-up on customer service and warranty matters?

Whatever segment of your business needs tightening up is where you should look to automate first. After all, when you spend the time and money to purchase, install and train yourself and your staff on a computer system, you want the quickest return on your investment. You want everyone to experience the improvement and the ability to increase output and accuracy of a specific task as only a computer can do.

If you already have a good manual accounting system, you can't improve your profitability by automating accounting and letting some area of your business continue to suffer.

The choices you have today in software give you a tremendous advantage over your competitors who computerized earlier and before the concepts of integration were introduced.

What is meant by the word "integration" in the context of the world of computers is that no matter what system you purchase today, you want to make sure you can in the future install your next program in a manner that will allow both or all future programs to "talk" to each other with single key-stroke operation. This is "integration" of the program language and is the mark of the most advanced systems you should be looking for.

The tasks of making materials lists, operating, designing, planning, managing, selling and customer service can all be computerized today. Property management, direct mailing and many other jobs can be done by computer. So, don't listen to the people when they want you to buy their accounting program as the first module in your computer system unless you are convinced that is the task you need most to have automated. Above all, get the assurance that the program you choose will integrate with other programs you might purchase in the future.

"Will it save me money? Will it make me money?" If the answer is anything other than an emphatic and unequivocal "yes," then look to another function to automate.

After deciding which part of your business you want to computerize first, chances are you will not find a program that does everything exactly as you wish. Therefore, it is essential that you know who you are doing business with. Will the software publisher guarantee the performance? Is the program flexible enough to allow you to make adjustments? Will the publisher support you with a toll-free telephone?

Choosing a company from which to purchase your computer software is much the same as selecting the products and materials you use to put into your homes. The companies with the best service, support and product warranties will give you the least trouble in the future. Use the same instincts to purchase your computer needs as you do your construction materials. You are a professional in product selection, and there is no mystique to buying computer products.

Don't let the fact that there are so many products and vendors to choose from confuse the main issues, which are.

1. Will the product do what you need done?
2. Will the company stand behind its product and support your needs?
3. Is the company reliable and have they been in business a long time?
4. Does the company understand your business or just the computer business?
5. Does the company offer a wide selection of computer programs for your industry so that when you want to add new programs you can continue to deal with them?
6. Will your program integrate with others when the time comes to add new capabilities?

Every program you purchase will take time to learn and meld into your current operation. Choosing the first element of your business to computerize should be carefully done so that you will cause the least disruption to the everyday operations while receiving the maximum benefit from what this amazing technology can do for you.

William R. Effinger has been a builder and developer for 30 years. He is a business consultant to the construction industry and chairman of Bird Construction Software.

101

Bill Effinger

friday, july 29, 1988 — New England Builders Edition — page be-five

Massachusetts Builders

By Bill Effinger, chairman, Bird Construction Software

Learn about all the technology available to the building industry

Part I of this article appeared in the June 24 issue of the Builders Edition.

The computer does in minutes what it would take a team of people weeks to do.

The element of time saving cannot be overlooked or given a less than "key" role in the decision-making department when you are considering purchasing a computer and software.

When deciding whether you need a computer to help manage your business more easily and allow you more free time, you should first examine the wide variety of jobs which are capable of being executed by the computer today.

Accounting is what most people consider as a logical computer function — which, of course, it is. However, there are many other facets of the business which can be enhanced through the use of this fantastic tool.

Consulting for builders and developers has given me the opportunity to see and discuss business applications for computers and to have several exciting programs demonstrated as they are used in the operating environment of a growing building business.

Over the past two years I have cataloged over 700 programs available to the construction industry. These range from a simple take-off program to highly sophisticated estimating systems incorporating a digitizer, scheduling systems utilizing plotters and CADD systems for every possible single-user application you can think of. There are dirt-balance and profile programs and literally hundreds of accounting programs being offered.

Listed below is some of the application software for the building industry currently being used by builders, developers and contractors:
- Accounts Payable
- Accounts Receivable
- General Ledger
- Payroll
- Job Costing

hardware and software. There is no hardware or software which exceeds the price of $1,000 on this list. I will be happy to supply you with the name of the product and a purchase source for any of the applications mentioned. Just send a self-addressed, stamped envelope to: W.R. Effinger, Suite 451, 346-348 Washington St., Braintree, MA 02184.

"But my operation is too small," I hear this over and over again. The truth of the matter is ... the smaller you are, the more you need to automate. Instead of coming home every night and working to the "wee hours" doing your estimating and bookkeeping and maybe using up Saturdays and Sundays as well, why not put the computer to work for you?

My brother is a successful small builder/developer in southern California, specializing in apartments. After a prolonged period of "should we or shouldn't we," he and his partner recently took the plunge and purchased an inexpensive IBM clone to do their property management and accounting. At dinner the other evening, he very proudly showed me his computer-generated occupancy reports, collection reports and delinquency reports, and then went on to tell me that it now only takes 3 hours to print the checks, post all of the accounts, print the reports and all schedules for 18 separate projects he now operates. This process would have taken more than 5 days of one person's time before the computer was installed.

Predictably, he is now looking to automate more functions of his business.

I recently wrote a preamble for a marketing package of software which puts a clear focus on the benefits of the computer. I will share it with you here to make my point.

I am looking for an
cont. on page be-18

Midland Wood Siding Sales
WOODSTOCK, CT.

- Many varieties of redwood and cedar for siding and trim in inventory.
- Competitive pricing and prompt delivery.
- Friendly, knowledgeable sales staff.
- Over 3,000,000 sq. ft. delivered in 1987 to Southern New England job sites.
- Call for a complete product listing in siding, decking and trim.

OUR TOLL FREE NUMBERS

In Ct. **1-800-962-0024**
Outside Ct. **1-800-762-0024**

NEW!

DECKING

Clear Cedar		Construciton Heart Redwood	
5/4 x 4	.47/Lin. Ft.	5¼x6	
5/4 x 6	.89/Lin. Ft.	2x4	
2 x 4	.80/Lin. Ft.	2x6	
2 x 6	1.65/Lin. Ft.	4x4	
4 x 4 - 8 ft. - 14.75/pce.			

If Your Product Isn't Selling — Maybe You Should Raise the Price!

by Bill Effinger

A 144-unit condominium project was built in the small coastal town of Del Mar, California. The developers had designed two types of products, hoping to capture the mid-range and higher-end buyer. After 14 months of advertising and sales activity, only 27 units had been sold and only 17 were closed. Several marketing firms were pooled for solutions and the exclusive right to sell the project for the owners. While each firm had their own unique approach to advertising and merchandising, they all were in agreement on one element of the problem—the price was too high for both products.

After being asked to tackle the problem, I spent some time with the salespeople reviewing the quality of the prospects, looking at all of the competition in the area, and analyzing the advertising they had used. Then I carefully walked the project and studied the price structure as the units related to each other for views, distance to parking and recreational facilities, etc. With this information in hand, I then made the recommendation to reprice all of the product and redirect the advertising to the high end of the product line rather than the low end as they had been doing.

We lowered some prices and raised some prices, but the net effect was an across-the-board increase of $10,000 per unit. We also changed the ads to target the buyer of the higher-priced homes by stating the mid-range sales prices of the upper-end product. Previously, they had been running the lowest priced unit in the lower-end product.

Immediately the quality of the traffic improved. With this strategy implemented, the sell-out of the remaining 117 units took less than a year. Why? How was it possible to sell more product by raising the price?

Good pricing strategy is made up of several elements, not the least of which is the psychology of the potential buyer. Establishing, lowering, or raising the price of a product requires more than knowing what it costs and how much profit you want to make. When you want a clue on how to price products, just spend some research time in the women's section of any department store and track some specific items for a period of time—you'll soon get the idea. Starting with how the departments are arranged and on to the "sale" racks, the appeal is to the impulse side of the buying equation. For an example that is closer to our industry, examine the results of a mortgage interest rate decrease. Most of the time your traffic and sales will slow down or stop altogether. Why? Because the buyer expects the rates to go down even further. Sales will rarely pick up again without some stimulus until the rates begin their inevitable climb. Then there's a rush to buy before it's too late. The same holds true when you start lowering your sales prices—the buyers will wait until they think you are at the bottom. If you don't know what your homes are worth, how can the buyer be expected to know?

The magic of correct pricing requires that you focus on the dreams, needs, and wants of the purchaser in addition to the demographic data you have on your product as it relates to them. Demographic data deals with the ideal conditions under which a prospect will execute a purchase. Location of the home or project, the size of the family, their income level and whether it's a dual- or single-wage earning family, and the occupation of the wage earner are all examples of demographic information.

Psychographics examines the motivations of the home buyer when considering the purchase. It is the process the buyer goes through to reach a final decision. Psychographics focuses on the impulse of the buyer at the point of sale. Compromises away from the demographic profile will occur in this mode. Will the purchase be considered mainly as an investment? Do they need more space? What are their "hot buttons?" Design? Value? Prestige? Function?

Successful advertising will always appeal to the psychographic side of the purchase decision. Successful pricing strategy should do the same. You want people going through your models who can afford to purchase what you have to sell, not those who wish they could buy but can't even qualify for the loan. Filling up the weekly traffic report with lookers isn't the goal—closing sales is what you and the sales staff want to accomplish.

You may have taken every step in your market plan to correctly identify your buyer profile, researched the competition and accurately costed your units, only to find that the prospects coming to your project either aren't qualified to buy or you don't even get a chance to sit them down. So—what's wrong, then?

Almost everyone will tell you that if you aren't selling, your price is too high. Right? That's what the sales force always tells you. W-e-l-l-l-l — lowering the price may not be the best approach. Maybe you should raise the price! Let's take a look at this alternative.

To help reach a conclusion as to what the proper solution might be, we need to consider what the available data has shown us about a typical home buyer relative to his or her motivation to purchase a new home.

First and foremost, they have a "dream." Next come some specific "wants," and finally there are definite needs. This "dream/want/need" list usually equates to

13

Back in San Diego after a leisurely cross country drive hauling my home as I went, I parked the fifth wheel in "Camp Land on The Bay" in a space about 100 feet from the boat launch and sandy beach, ready to soak up some California sun and get to work rebuilding my consulting business.

But I got sidetracked; living the single life for several years and leaving a relationship in Boston with a remarkable woman, I was ready for something permanent.

Thanks to my brother's wife Diane Effinger, who introduced me to who is now my outstanding friend and life partner, my wife Diana. Our first date was a sail aboard my brother's sloop. When he gave the tiller to Diana and she handled the boat like she had been sailing her whole life, it was love at first sail!

Marriage took a while, however; As a matter of fact—a long while; 6-years to be exact. In the process we covered a great deal of geography having great fun along the way.

***

Confessions of a Serial Entrepreneur

Fine Line Creations, Steamboat Springs, Colorado

Always wanting to own her own business, Diana joined her longtime friend writer-artist, Lynne, moved up to Steamboat Springs Colorado and opened an art gallery they named "Four Directions" featuring sundry items covering a multitude of artistic genre—I followed her with my fifth wheel, settling in a travel trailer park on the Yampa river just outside of town.

Having nothing to do while there, I dipped into my creative bag and reasonable artistic talent, designing hand drawn greeting cards, "T" Shirts and Sweat shirts with designs related to Steamboat Springs' reputation for skiing, hunting and fishing.

First, I wanted and needed some income. Idleness isn't in my makeup, so I took a part time job in the local "Ace Hardware Store" and another in a gift store—two days a week in each. That left three days, so I created the company"'Fine Line Creations" and enticed local stores to sell my shirts, cards and wire sculptures.

Original Art

by

Local Artist

Bill Effinger

Produced and sold by:
Fine Line Creations
Steamboat Springs, Colorado

Bill Effinger

Diana and I spent our leisure times bathing in the local natural hot water springs and sampling the simple carefree life of resort living—great fun for two years, but when the business Diana and her friend started wasn't grossing what they felt they needed to survive, they closed it down and we headed south to San Diego once again.

First however, I gave all of my shirt designs to the Imprinter who had been stenciling the shirts for me. I was told many years later, that they were still selling, particularly the shirts depicting the "Cowboy Downhill Race"; one of the most popular yearly events in Steamboat Springs.

We were happy to have had the experience, but equally happy to be back in the land of the eternal sun.

Retailers Of Our Products

Off The Beaten Path

Tread of the Pioneers Museum

The Shirt Stop

Santa Fe Art Co.

Soda Creek Mercantile

Design Of The Times

Coldwell Banker / Silver Oak Ltd.

Franklin Mall

Seltzer Mortgage

Mical Mortgage

Main Street Coffee House

Bill Effinger

Where I sat and made Wire sculptures and hung for sale

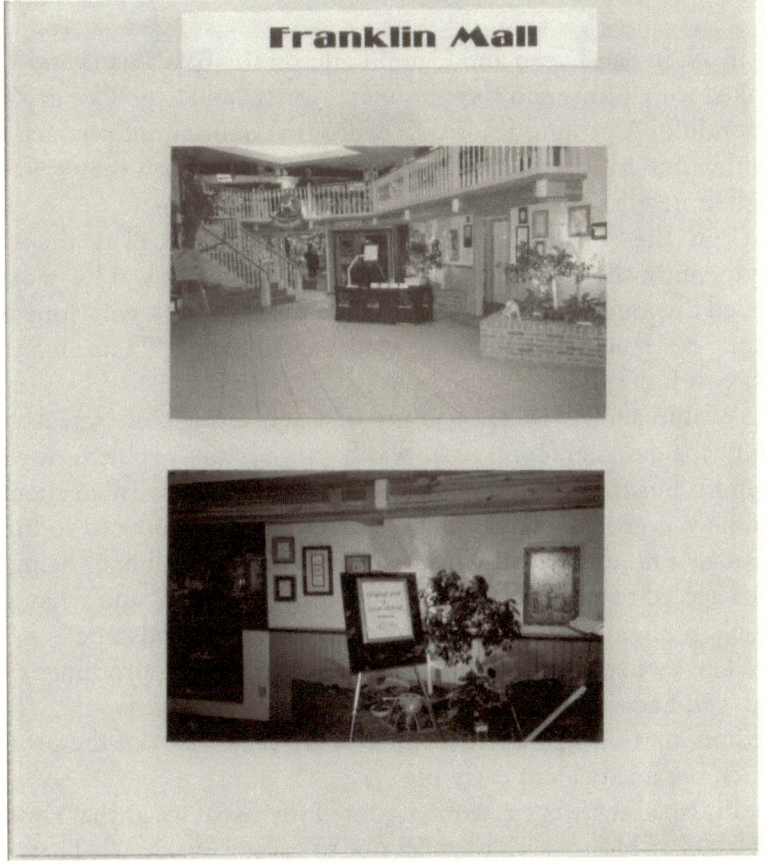

I explained to Diana as she and her friend closed down their business, "there are no failures in an entrepreneurial venture, only learning experiences". I often tell my clients that one of the reasons I am very good as a business consultant is because of all of the experiences making mistakes in my own businesses.

I am proud to wear the mantle of a "serial entrepreneur" with the twenty-one businesses I have founded and shared in this business memoire.

WRE Consultant (again)

Back in San Diego and Camp Land on the Bay, Diana and I looked for a home and found one in North San Diego County's Escondido; A ground floor two bedroom condominium which my brother and his partner had taken in on a trade when they sold one of their newly constructed homes.

I put the Ford truck and fifth wheel up for sale, made the down payment on the condo and we moved in. Diana looked for work and landed one quickly at Scripps Institute in La Jolla—a very long drive. I hung my real estate license in Paul Van Elderen's "Hanson Realty" office in Escondido.

Within a few weeks, I had my first consulting contract: A young landscape designer/contractor was having serious problems trying to keep his business going even though he had many satisfied clients and he was grossing large dollar volume. I was introduced to him through a mutual friend who suggested I might be able to help.

I agreed to meet and take a look at his operation and what the problem might be. The company was "Natures Landscape".

The owner was in his late twenties, the son of a prominent local and well know wellness-doctor and his brother was his accountant/financial advisor—that, was a major part of the problem which became evident early on.

Finished with my review, I quoted my usual fee at that time, $250.00 Per Hour, with the cost not to exceed $6,000.00. The young man thought that was too steep, so I said "you will get what you pay for and I am so confident that if I haven't helped solve your problem, you won't have to pay me anything". He agreed to the deal and I began the next morning to suggest the changes he needed to make, which were many.

Within ninety days we had made changes to his operation which ultimately turned his business around to being very profitable by year's end. Being on the brink of going out of business and then to turn a real bankable profit, my client was quite happy and I received my $6,000.00—end of story.

I managed to get a write-up about the turnaround in the local paper, which resulted in my next consulting assignment.

Confessions of a Serial Entrepreneur

Cutting root problems saves landscaping firm

KATHY DAY
NORTH COUNTY TIMES

ESCONDIDO — Steve Jacobs knew if he didn't do something quickly, his Nature Designs would fail.

A landscape contractor who started his company in 1983, he'd seen the books. He knew what started as the losing trend in 1994 had snowballed in the first quarter of 1995.

He lost jobs he should have won.

His brother, Dave, an accountant, told him he was in trouble.

But until he met Bill Effinger, he avoided the issue.

Jim Felix, a friend from Escondido's Country Club Kiwanis group, introduced the pair at lunch, where they were joined by another landscape contractor, who had maintained Jacobs' father's home for years.

Effinger, who formerly ran Shappell Industries' San Diego operation, now works as a business turnaround consultant and motivational speaker, said he has seen lots of small companies in the same situation as Jacobs'.

"Steve was distraught," he said. "He was laying out his heart to a stranger. He'd borrowed money from his dad and brother, even a client."

From that first meeting, Effinger knew that Jacobs loved landscaping but didn't like to manage. "It was typical. They'd seen a big increase in business and a net decrease in profits. He didn't know how he'd lost $40,000."

Effinger asked Jacobs some questions, told him that his fee was probably more than Jacobs would likely consider paying, considering the state of his business, and told him he would work

Nature Designs operations director Mike Cox, owner Steve Jacobs and consultant Bill Effinger inspect a horse jumping area which the company designed for an Olivenhain homeowner.

JAMIE SCOTT LYTLE/ NORTH COUNTY TIMES

▶ ROOT, D-2

Meanwhile, an affordable housing developer, Jim Silverwood, was rapidly growing his successful business, "Affirmed Housing Group, Inc." Jim had recently hired a young woman who he felt had great promise for his company. He asked if I would consider mentoring her to help smooth out some rough edges in her management style.

111

The assignment has ended up being a twenty five year business and friendly relationship with Affirmed Housing and the young lady I was asked to mentor so many years ago. Today she is the owner of her own multifaceted businesses, one of them being an affordable housing developer. "Hitzke Development Corporation".

My consulting function with Affirmed and ultimately Hitzke Development was to spot the right properties for their projects, help negotiate the acquisition, and then help shepherd the projects through the approval process with the municipalities in which the projects were located.

Both companies kept me quite busy and well compensated, but I needed more to keep me busy. My association with Paul Van Elderen and Hanson Realty provided action and the income as I sold and leased properties listed with the real estate company.

My largest and most long lasting consulting assignment was with a Dutch friend/entrepreneur of Van Elderen's, Dolf Scherpbier, Scherpbier owned a very large 130 acre parcel of land within a 250 acre parcel owned by fifteen other owners. The property was assigned the name "Quail Hills" and planned as an industrial site that for more than 16 years. The property had never received the approval from the City of Escondido to go forward with its ultimate development and construction.

I spent seven years and six months keeping all sixteen property owners on the same page, while I relentlessly pursued and ultimately received the needed approvals to develop the site.

Today the completed site is the home of the famous "Stone Brewery Bottling Plant" and tourist destination restaurant; The newest and most modern, $2.5Billion Dollar Hospital in America, "Palomar Medical Center"; a major power plant owned by "Sempra Energy"; several industrial buildings occupied by sundry companies and a soon-to-be- constructed hotel which will be owned and operated by Stone Brewery owners.

The result for me was one of the largest consulting fees I had ever collected, and watching every one of the sixteen property owners become happy campers, as they deposited checks in their respective banks.

Confessions of a Serial Entrepreneur

ESCONDIDO ---- Low-income housing has not only offered Escondido-based Affirmed Housing Group an untapped market in North County, but also has supplied the company with a fan club. While giving a tour of one of his projects Tuesday, Affirmed Housing President James "Jim" Silverwood was interrupted by a resident at the Ventaliso Apartments in San Marcos, who enthusiastically heaped him with compliments and thanks for providing affordable rents for herself and her daughter.

"Seeing reactions like that really makes this a great experience," Silverwood said. "Not only are we, as a company, able to be successful building affordable homes, but we have this extra benefit of empowering people and giving them a better life."

Affirmed, which has operated in Escondido since the company opened in 1994, is resurfacing again as one of several developers answering the city's request for proposals to build housing in the city's urban core. Silverwood, who has two other low-income projects in Escondido and projects in the works from San Diego to Murrieta, has declined to release the details of the new low-income proposal until the final plans are submitted to the city next week.

Silverwood's foray into the low-income housing market started in the early 1990s after he faced a lack of capital for regular housing developments and a sluggish housing industry, he said. A long time residential housing developer, Silverwood formed Affirmed and turned his attention to low-income housing, learning how to use city money and federal and state tax credits to secure financing to build lower-rent apartments. "It is a complicated and cumbersome process," he said. "The most significant barrier is the financing. It is particularly complex because there are multiple layers of funding needed."

Since low-income apartments do not bring in as much money as complexes with higher rents, Affirmed must secure more funding from different sources. Those other sources are usually governmental funding, which requires painstakingly-detailed documentation, a deterrent to many home developers, he said. But Affirmed has thrived, producing $100 million in affordable housing developments across the country, with 566 units in Southern California and 350 units outside the state, said Ginger Hitzke, Affirmed's senior project manager. The residents pay rent based on their family size and income, she added.

Bill Effinger

Locally, Affirmed has developed four projects in North County: two in Escondido and two in San Marcos. Along with Ventaliso, a new 48-unit apartment complex, Affirmed's first project partnering with the city of San Marcos was to renovate a 70-unit apartment formally called San Marcos Gardens, said Charlie Schaffer, San Marcos' development services director.

"Affirmed turned an old dilapidated apartment complex into a renovated project that was instrumental in turning the whole neighbourhood around," Schaffer said. "Now, there has been a lot of new developments, the crime rate has dropped, and it has been a real positive for the city. Affirmed Housing Group was a big part of that." Affirmed has two projects under construction in San Diego. To fight off stereotypes of low-income residents being problem-tenants, Affirmed requires extensive background checks on its applicants.

"We do it because we don't want the neighbourhood to have issues with our tenants," Silverwood said. "If a tenant objects to the check, there is always the next person on the waiting list." But judging from the amount of fan mail Affirmed receives, the tenants don't seem to mind Affirmed's careful checking: "I feel lucky to have been accepted into this complex," wrote Raquel Carr, a single mother of two who lives in Affirmed's The Terraces in Escondido. "The Terraces have been a big part of my life and the changes I've made to better it."

Contact staff writer Erin Massey at (760) 740-5416. 9/11/02

❖❖❖

Stone Brewery and Restauraant, Escondido CA

Bill Effinger

Stone Brewery Production and Bottling Facility Escondido, CA

Palomar Medical Center, Escondido CA

I formed New Century Consulting in 2008 after leaving Hanson Realty and rented a space in an Executive Suite facility across from San Marcos City Hall where I was currently performing most of my consulting work with Affirmed and Hitske. My oldest son Kirk joined me shortly thereafter seeking new clients.

New Century Consulting

Once settled in the new office, we began working on finding new clients and servicing our current clients.

I had just completed assisting my client Hitzke Development in acquiring a foreclosed 60-unit condo project from the FDIC, in Desert Hot Springs, which she needed some help from the city, so I tended to that issue with some city council friends I had generated while living there.

Then both clients, Hitzke and Affirmed, were having trouble with the "Valicitos Water District" in San Marcos, as were several other building and contracting companies. I had long standing relationships with past and current management of the District, so I represented both companies on the issues they had.

Following that, Affirmed asked me to assist them in the acquisition of a commercial property is San Marcos, which kept me busy for several months in the process. I was negotiating with the owners and the city, because the city was putting up the funds to acquire the site for an affordable housing project.

We ended up with a $3.2million price tag, and a nice commission for me. That project is just now in the completion stage, five-years since acquisition. Even with city funding, the approval process burns up months and years of precious time and money.

***

My wife was soon retiring from her position with the "University of California", and began talking about wanting to move close to her daughter in Washington State. My youngest son lives in Vancouver Washington, so adventurers that we are, we started a search to find a home up there.

My first step was to apply for a "Washington Real Estate License", there is reciprocity between California and Washington, so I didn't need to attend their school, but it would require my taking a test which I did.

Then I joined the "Kitsap Home Builders Association", so I could hit the ground running whenever we moved there.

My goal for after we settled on a home, was to convince my clients to build some affordable housing on the "Kitsap Peninsula" which were badly needed.

We continued operating out of that office until we decided to move north to Washington State so my wife Diana could fulfill her wish to be closer to her daughter Linda and her family. Since my youngest son Brian, his wife Mindy and four of her siblings were living in Vancouver Washington, as was his daughter Heather and her husband, we would be close to them as well.

With Linda and her husband, we began our search near them in Silverdale which is fast becoming the economic hub of Kitsap County.

We searched on the web while Linda and Glenn followed up with a physical drive by, sending us their thoughts and pictures.

After house shopping close to Linda and her husband Glenn, we decided on a new home that would be built in the small new community of "Chateau Ridge" in the historic city of "Poulsbo" situated on the tip of "Liberty Bay on Kitsap Peninsula", where we currently reside. I had hopes of consulting here but that hasn't taken place as yet.

Kitsap Peninsula is on the west side of the sound where the "Naval Shipyard in Bremerton" and several communities are growing, though hit hard by the real estate bust of 2008.

During February 2013, we purchased the home to be constructed and finished by July.

We moved in on July 22nd, 2013 and after getting settled, I began scouring the area for possible sites to build some multi-density affordable housing, and meeting as many professionals in the industry as quickly as I could. For that, I went to some meetings at the Kitsap HBA, where I quickly learned that I was in an area which in the words of a local Title Officer: "is 25-years behind California or more"—not good news, to be sure.

I have introduced myself to the business and construction communities, joined and become an active member of the "Poulsbo Rotary", had several op-ed pieces published in the local paper on housing and government and have developed relationships with several builders and contractors.

I have unsuccessfully made three attempts to put affordable housing projects together for my two clients because the cities and county lack funding to help in the effort as we have come to expect in California, where both clients continue unabated in building such projects throughout the state.

Thoroughly disappointed, but determined, my eyes continue to remain open for possible opportunities. Should one appear, I will follow the lead to where it takes me as always.

Meanwhile, my hobby of writing will have to satisfy my need to stay active.

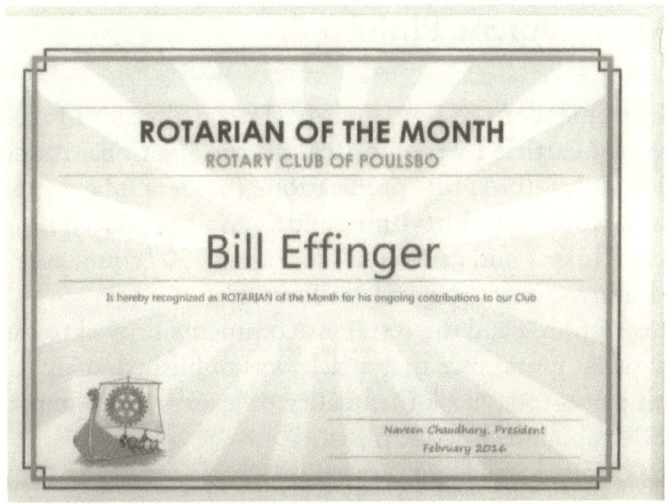

Historic Downtown Poulsbo's Front Street

My Management Philosophy

The tremendous response received from a recent LinkedIn posting of an article I wrote in 1990 for the "National Association of Home Builders' (NAHB)" publication "Builders' Management Journal". More than thirty-thousand "views" produced nearly four-thousand "Likes" and generated more than 350 "comments" and created more than a thousand "followers".

This response and the resultant comments proved to me those twenty-seven years since that article was published, many managers in work places today lack the quality of leadership so important in the modern high-tech work place.

The original article follows:

The Best Way to Manage People is Don't

Lead people, guide them: educate them, set examples for them, but don't try to manage them. Establish priorities for people, schedule tasks and projects with them, review progress and achievements with them, help them set goals, but don't try to manage them.

The best managers are not managers, they are facilitators. You know who they are. They are the owners and supervisors of highly successful companies with motivated employees and good reputations with customers, suppliers, and subcontractors. Their companies always seem to be on top of the competition with more jobs, better clients, and high profits. How do they do it? Let's examine some of the methods that have proven to be the most effective in the office and in the field.

Be a coach: I have always found that the most effective method for directing people is to assume the role of a coach. A good coach starts with the premise that his team members are professionals, which they have winning attitudes and the desire to perform to the best of their ability. So it should be with your employees or subcontractors. If they don't have these qualities, then they shouldn't be hired. As professionals, all they need is a good game plan and the flexibility to make adjustments in the how to accomplish what in the most productive and effective way.

State your expectations and insist on commitment: The most important criteria for getting a high-quality product in the most profitable fashion is to make sure that the people responsible for providing it understand what is expected of them. They must be committed to the task. This commitment can only be determined by the initial contact between the supervisor and the employee, either in the selection process (in the case of a new hire), or during the project planning discussion in a pre-job conference.

Provide scheduled delivery times: By preparing a detailed schedule for starting and ending the project, you let employees or subcontractors know that the element of time is vitally important to the satisfactory completion of the task. You also confirm that they understand your expectations.

Set performance criteria: After you explain what the task is, the level of quality you expect, and the time allotted to perform the task, make it very clear what you will expect as acceptable performance. Don't tell a professional how to do the job unless he or she specifically asks for recommendations or clarifications. Then, of course, provide the necessary information to help him or her understand.

Be communicative and request positive feedback: Reassuring your people that you believe they are professionals takes you halfway to a successful operation. By maintaining good communication with them, you will be kept sufficiently informed of their progress to establish that everything is running smoothly without having them feel that you are "checking up" on them or "second guessing" them. A good coach asks, "How are you doing, John?" instead of "What are you doing, John?"

Frequent but brief meetings (5 to 10 minutes) in the field and in the office can prove beneficial for both you and the employees, but only if both sides expect and provide honest, direct information and feedback on prior sessions. Each person must feel free to discuss any past or current decisions and the possible negative effects that those decisions may have on the overall progress or quality of the job.

A weekly meeting with the entire production and support group, lasting no longer than one hour, will help everyone better understand the whole picture of progress and profitability.

Apply mutual goal-setting techniques: Helping employees "go beyond themselves" is possibly the most rewarding thing that a supervisor can do for both himself and the employees. Nudging and guiding people to take bold steps can reap some very positive and unexpected results when the task is correctly understood. Each person is monitored for achievement of the goal and assisted in a limited way to help him or her reach the goals. Of course, the process is not without risk. This is where leadership takes form.

Show leadership: A good leader will allow his or her team members to make mistakes. This is how they grow. I don't mean you should just ignore a mistake, but you allow it to happen without severe reprimand. The important thing to understand is that when the mistake is made, it should be calmly pointed out. Possible solutions should be discussed right then and there, allowing the employee to become part of the solution to the problem that he or she created. The task then ends on a "high note" rather than one of incompetence or dissatisfaction.

Give positive reinforcement: "Atta boys" can never be too frequent. The good coach is always giving positive strokes to the team members. Every job has its tedium. Some encouragement now and then helps make the task easier, and workers who feel valued take more pride in their work. A good leader passes all of the applause and recognition from senior management right on to the team members, but shields them from ridicule or embarrassment. A good leader prepares the team for the unexpected but is willing to take the flak for them if there is a foul-up. Mistakes will happen. They should be discussed and analyzed, in a calm and rational way, to see how they can be avoided in the future.

Be a positive role model: Naturally, setting good examples for employees when it comes to timeliness, order, and quality control in day-to-day tasks is essential to good leadership. You can hardly expect your employees to be on time if you are always late, or to be organized and quality conscious if you are not.

Keep a sense of perspective: A good sense of humor and the willingness to share some levity with your subordinates can keep an otherwise difficult problem or task in perspective. I don't mean that you should be telling jokes all day. But the job needs to be dealt with on a level that allows some comic relief from extreme pressures. Otherwise, everyone may grow tense and lose sight of one of the goals—to enjoy what they are doing.

Imply "ownership": Having pride in the product being delivered to the consumer is probably one of the most important elements of a well-directed team. Your employees and subcontractors must believe in what they are doing and be proud to say, "I helped build that." A sense of "ownership" is a meaningful accomplishment for a professional; it transcends the monetary element of the overall goals for the individual.

Stress accountability: Accountability for actions and decisions is essential for employees to fully understand what is expected of them. They must have the sense of ownership in the end result or product in order to fully appreciate the importance of their efforts in the overall scheme of things. By making employees fully responsible for their actions, you help them to improve themselves. This, in turn, will improve their performance, increasing production effectiveness and quality control.

Encourage continuing education: The more educated and informed your people are, the better and more effective decisions they will make. The current availability of seminars, courses, classes, informative trade association magazines and newsletters can improve the level of employee performance and feeling of self-worth beyond measure. Your people should be encouraged and, if financially feasible, assisted in attending as many of these sessions as possible. Naturally, the most desirable educational opportunities should focus on a specific job-oriented topic related to the position they hold with your company. Professional recognition or status (such as COR or MIRM) can be both beneficial and rewarding to the recipients as well as the company. This type of educational programming improves relationships because of the level of understanding achieved in the process.

In summary a successful manager: *manages a business* but *works with people* in a free-flowing exchange of ideas, effort, and integrity. The manager provides positive reinforcement as often as possible. The manager who becomes mentor by example and deed to his crew, team, or group will reap personal satisfaction and monetary rewards through better quality products and more efficient systems, and drive the bottom line of the business to new heights.

©1990

It's a Family Thing—several family members are also entrepreneurs:

My oldest son Kirk after spending more than 20-years in the Mortgage origination business, founded and published two magazines and published them in San Marcos and Escondido California for 3 & 4-years then sold them to the respective cities' Chamber of Commerce. He is currently in the Real Estate business.

Coincidently, Kirk serves on the Foundation Board of Palomar Hospital in Escondido, referred to earlier in this manuscript as my having been instrumental in its approval and construction on the site which I processed through the City of Escondido's approval.

My second oldest son, Lynn, has been involved in the housing and mortgage servicing industries for nearly four decades.

Among other positions, he has served as Vice President-REO Manager for three of the nation's largest mortgage lenders. He has also been an entrepreneur in his own right, serving as publisher and editor of Escondido Magazine, principal of Effinger & Associates, a regional advertising and public relations agency in Southern California serving builders, developers, real estate companies and mortgage lenders.

Lynn is also the former producer and host of "Real Estate Matters," a weekly radio talk show in San Diego.

Most recently, Lynn has served as an independent consultant to various national firms within the mortgage servicing industry. He has also served as an expert moderator and panelist at various industry conferences and seminars across the country over the past two decades, as well as having various articles published in several mortgage industry trade journals, magazines and online publications.

Additionally, Lynn travels to paid appearances around the country as a motivational speaker. His book 'Believe to Achieve – The Power of Perseverance,' is available on Amazon.com, Barnes and Noble.com and other online outlets, and has received numerous accolades.

My youngest son Brian, retired from the Navy many years ago, went right back to serving our country as a civilian doing the very important job of managing a team in the Naval recruitment center in Portland, Oregon, and applying his entrepreneurial skills to help revamp the system.

"I wouldn't consider myself much of an entrepreneur, But I've certainly earned my stripes as an analyst, mediator, trainer, mentor, and partner in shaping the most well-rounded and respected NRPS among the 65 in the system. If I were to take a poll I'd bet I have earned more Gold Wreaths than any recruiter or civilian in CNRC (64)."

My Daughter Valerie Stoddard created the first High School weather station in the U. S. in Steamboat Springs Colorado; she is an accomplished artist, has sold many of her paintings and glassware pieces.

My granddaughter Kelly Fox has had her own very successful graphic design business for several years in San Marcos California.

My granddaughter Heather Walters has recently started a graphic design business in Vancouver Washington.

Heather's Husband Burton is in the Real Estate business, also in Vancouver Washington.

Confessions of a Serial Entrepreneur

My granddaughter Chelsie Bunnell has her own successful online Etsy business.

My Grandson's Wife Meghan Effinger is the exclusive seller of the popular 'Barefoot Books' children's book publisher.

My wife Diana had her own business in Steamboat Springs Colorado in 1992/93 before we moved back to San Diego. 'Four Directions' was an art gallery featuring a wide variety of art objects and paintings.

***

Bill Effinger

Summary of Challenges, Mistakes & Triumphs

Speedy Quick Delivery Service: 1950

Lesson learned—research your idea before implementing it and investing time, effort and finances. Mistakes in business ventures can be costly and hard to recover from. This was not a failed business, it was a lesson learned and shared.

Boulevard Saw Shop: 1950-1952

Lesson learned: Owning your own business is fun, profitably rewarding and hard work. Know your market, get to know your clients and serve them well; they will continue to use your services and most likely recommend you to others.

W.R. Effinger Rough Framing Company 1952-1956

Lesson learned: When opportunity knocks, do your homework; assess the opportunity for what it is, read the fine print. Should the contract you are being asked to sign have clauses you don't understand, seek legal advice and proceed with caution. Should the need for legal advice arise at some point in the execution of your contract, make sure the lawyer or law firm you engage, has specific experience in the type of issue you are confronted with.

Decca Investors Inc. Dissolved: 1957-1958

My experience of buying and selling land for the past 70-years has shown that when purchasing real estate, especially land, and the zoning changes from a long standing dormant condition such as agricultural to commercial the value rises instantly to its highest and best use value. From that point on, the value will only rise relative to the general economy and inflation.

I have given seminars on this subject to land owners and Real Estate professionals.

S & S Construction Company Land Buyer

Lessons learned: The owner of the company, Nathan Shapell allowed me to seek my own level of responsibility while never allowing accountability to wane, which proved to me that when you are eager to learn and not fearful of making mistakes, positive things will happen for you.

The result was that I applied that philosophy to all of my future endeavors.

W.R. Effinger Designer Builder 1957-61: Rolled into Alamitos Belmont Corp.

Lesson Learned: I plunged into my new business with the usual gusto and abandon that up to now had typified my life—I knew what I wanted to do, I felt I knew the market I was going to be building for and I knew where I was going to build my first products.

Everything fell into place with such ease; I didn't appreciate it at the time. The more buildings I constructed, the more I sold and the more I sold, the growth of the business was remarkable.

In retrospect, what I should have done was stop, take a breath and make a plan for the future—something I helped many of my clients do after I learned the lesson of hyper growth.

Community Plaza-Long Beach California

Lesson Learned: There are opportunities where others have not gone or have passed up. When things look difficult or maybe even impossible, the rewards for persistence and perseverance can be beyond your imagination. Follow your dream.

Rancho Valencia: 234-unit Garden Apartment complex 1966-71: Relinquished

Lesson Learned: In retrospect and using the 40-plus years of experience I have had since this bump in the road, I had way too many balls in the air at the same time. While each of my diverse businesses were profitable each took some of my attention away from my primary business, which was building and development.

I couldn't foresee the S & L doing what they did when they did it, but walking away and leaving them with the unfinished project would have been the smart thing to do.

I could have filed Bankruptcy on that project and left the S & L the problem, and protected all the other businesses by transferring ownership to a separate corporation—it's done all the time. Like they say, 'hind sight is always 20-20.

Valencia Liquors

Lesson Learned: Follow your instincts, and only listen to professionals who represent the buying public rather than the companies they represent when selling you their products. Market researchers, local newspapers magazines, radio and TV ads are good sources, but there is nothing like good old fashioned asking questions of your friends, neighbors and associates on what they would like to see and experience in your product.

Being different than your competition does have its rewards.

Huntington Harbor Liquors

Lesson Learned: When ideas seem crazy to everyone you know and the people of experience in your field of endeavor, caution you on the mistakes you are making, it's ok to stop and listen; but many times the probability of your success lies within those negative, cautionary and well-meaning Comments.

Examples abound of "You can't do that" being overcome as doubters look on in awe: Landing men on the moon, the I-Phone, the Internet—I could fill several pages with examples.

Dare to be different!

Blue Bird Nursery

There are times, when ignoring your inner self to meet another challenge becomes the best decision—the idea was a good one, but adding another challenge to my already full plate was over the top when I needed all of my attention to try to save my sinking ship.

My Ten Years with Shapell Industries

Lesson Learned: When someone throws you a lifeline, grab it and hold on...there is no shame in allowing someone to come to your rescue when your boat is sinking. Next time, you may be the person throwing the lifeline. What goes around comes around in this life. And remember, there is no failure, just lessons learned for the next venture.

New Dimensions for Living

Lesson Learned: Corporations are not 'people' as our current Supreme Court has ruled in the 'Citizens United' case for campaign finance. A corporation has no conscience, nor honor. A corporation is a vehicle for people to hide behind with a shrug of their shoulders and a "that's business" comment.

I learned the hard way that a 'letter of intent' is just that a statement that one party intends to (but is not obligated to) do whatever the two parties have discussed.

Seek legal advice when dealing with any corporation no matter how large or small, or how long they have been in business.

Techno Data

Lessons learned: While keeping your head down and plowing forward in your venture, don't forget to look up and take a long look at your competition and the changes that are probably occurring in the industry you are involved with.

In my case, the leap from a world of comparatively slow moving hammer and nails, boards and concrete, to a digital

world that was on its way to establishing 'Moore's Law' where everything doubles itself every two years, became a prophetic experience as I partnered with a 200-year old company.
<u>Bird Construction Software</u>

We were behind the curve of the digital revolution the day we started; we just didn't know it—at least this time we were spending Bird's money, not mine—that much, I learned since my first experience with them.

***

Afterword

Keeping with the main message of this book: one of the most important lessons of entrepreneurship, has nothing to do with starting or managing a particular business, but the rudiments of personal finance and the acquired discipline of adhering to a personal/family budget that will provide for the future in the event of something not quite going the way things might have been planned.

I did not have that attribute. When one business failed to meet expectations for whatever reason, rather than stepping back, taking a deep breath, and conserving what financial gains I had managed to salvage, I put everything on the line in the next venture—in short, my confidence in my ability to make the next venture succeed, overshadowed the common sense of "keeping something for a rainy day". This I have found to be a common trait among fellow Entrepreneurs and most of my clients.

Retrospectively, the result was always a financial win/lose scenario where the future was based on the success of the next venture, while exciting for me, was cataclysmic for my family; something I do not recommend.

Instead of buying and amassing a voluminous inventory of 'man toys' which I did have many, putting some cash in the bank would have served my, and my family's future much better.

Creating successful ventures is very self-satisfying, but there is an element of: "Why am I doing this?" In my case, amassing wealth had never been part of my interest. I was always so focused on the 'creating and doing' that the money was incidental to the goals—of course that was an imprudent outlook.

I have lived a full and adventurous life in business and life in general and have much to be thankful for. The successes and setbacks helped mold my education in what to do and not to do which has provided me with mountains of experiences to share with my consulting clients—an out of the ordinary education not otherwise gained without the doing.

Bill Effinger

Becoming an Entrepreneur is not for the faint of heart.
Entrepreneur:
A person who organizes and operates a business or businesses, taking on greater than normal financial risks in order to do so.
--**Webster's Dictionary**

***

"This defines entrepreneur and entrepreneurship - the entrepreneur always searches for change, responds to it, and exploits it as an opportunity."
— **Peter F. Drucker**

"I can honestly say that I have never gone into any business purely to make money. If that is the sole motive then I believe you are better off not doing it. A business has to be involving, it has to be fun, and it has to exercise your creative instincts."
— **Richard Branson**

"Entrepreneurship rests on a theory of economy and society. The theory sees change as normal and indeed as healthy. And it sees the major task in society - and especially in the economy - as doing something different rather than doing better what is already being done. That is basically what Say, two hundred years ago, meant when he coined the term entrepreneur. It was intended as a manifesto and as a declaration of dissent: the entrepreneur upsets and disorganizes. As Joseph Schumpeter formulated it, his task is "creative destruction."
— **Peter F. Drucker**

Author Bill Effinger

Bill lives in Poulsbo Washington with his wife Diana. They have six children, 16 grandchildren and 13 greatgrandchildren. .

www.ingramcontent.com/pod-product-compliance
Lightning Source LLC
Chambersburg PA
CBHW030806180526
45163CB00003B/1164